★★★★★

# BEEF SECRETS

*straight from the*

## BUTCHER

*by* **Lee O'Hara**

published by

**PRECISION WORDAGE PRESS**

Pasadena, CA

Published by **Precision Wordage Press**
a division of Precision Wordage Inc
PO Box 94536
Pasadena, CA 91109
www.precisionwordage.com

Cover design www.RonPereira.com

Concise Guidelines is a registered trademark owned exclusively by Precision Wordage Inc.

Published in the United States of America

First printing January 2010

ISBN 0-9627090-1-8

## About the *Concise Guidelines* Series

"All it takes a little common sense and a few concise guidelines." The Concise Guidelines Series is designed to provide workable data for your life. For great blogs and a list of other publications available in the series, please visit www.conciseguidelines.com.

## About MeatBasics101.com

For more information on beef and other meats, please visit the author's website www.meatbasics101.com.

## Disclaimer

To the Reader: Nothing in this book is intended to imply that all the ordinary rules of safe food and equipment handling don't apply, or shouldn't be followed at all times when handling beef or equipment. Fresh meat and perishable foods cannot be considered "safe" if they are kept for four hours or more at temperatures between $40^0$ F and $140^0$ F.

No promotional fees of any kind were paid, promised or anticipated in the publication of this book.

## Dedication

This book is dedicated to you,
the reader, with the hope that
you and yours will benefit
greatly from whatever you
might learn in the reading of it.

# About Me and Meat

My interest in meats started in 1958, when as a junior in high school, I got an after-school job as a cleanup boy at Green's Locker Service in Elk Grove, CA. Locker plants were common during the 1930s and into the 1960s, before home freezers became affordable and commonplace.

In those days, when a much higher percentage of the populace lived on small farms and many people raised their own meat, a butcher would go to the farm and slaughter the steer, pig or lamb right in the field. From there, the butcher would bring the animal to the locker plant where it would be skinned, quartered, and cooled until it was time for the carcass to be cut, wrapped and frozen according to the owner's instructions.

After the meat was "quick frozen," meaning that it was put in a freezer room that was kept between $-15^0$ to $-25^0$ Fahrenheit, it was either taken home by the customer, or the meat was put in the locker the customer had rented. Locker plant customers could go into the plant at any time it was open, walk into the very large "walk-in" freezer and put their fruits and vegetables or their meat in their individual frozen food locker or take it out as needed.

The locker plant had been closed for some years prior to Burt Green buying it and re-starting the business. It was just Burt, a part-time meat wrapper, and I who worked there.

I quickly learned how to trim the meat for wrapping, learned the cuts so they could be properly labeled, and learned to wrap the meat for freezing. Soon I was breaking the quarters of beef into the various sections, called primal cuts, and learning how to cut steaks and chops.

By the time I graduated from high school in 1960, the owner of the plant said that I was as good a meat cutter as any he could hire from the Meat Cutters Union Hall, and kept me on as an apprentice. This was for the first year of what was then the required two-year apprenticeship prior to earning the designation of "journeyman meat cutter."

After completing the first year of apprenticeship, with his influence, I was hired at Arata Brothers, which at the time was the largest volume super market in Sacramento, CA. The meat department employed eight full-time meat cutters, including me, and I was put on the "steak table" along with Clyde, a middle-aged meat cutter with over thirty years in the trade. Our responsibility was to do nothing but cut all the steaks and tend to the self-serve steak counter. Fifty to sixty hindquarters and fifty to sixty front quarters of beef were delivered to the store every Monday morning and broken into their primal cuts (round, head loin, short loin, rib, chuck, cross rib, flank and sirloin tip) by the end of the day. Unheard of by today's norms, the store was open only from Tuesday through Saturday, 9 A.M. to 6 P.M. From Tuesday through Saturday, Clyde and I did nothing but cut steaks and keep the steak counter full.

After becoming a journeyman, I had to leave Arata Brothers to be able to work part-time and take day classes at City and Sacramento State College.

I had attended night classes after graduating from high school but was more interested in continuing my education than contemplating being a meat cutter for the rest of my life. I worked out of the Union Hall. That meant that whenever a meat cutter called in sick or didn't show up for work, the boss could call the Hall and ask for a meat cutter to be sent to his store. Sometimes this was for one day's work, and sometimes it could turn into a regular part-time job.

For long periods during those school years I worked for Safeway, Raley's, Lucky's, Mayfair and a host of smaller chains and independent supermarkets on a part-time basis whenever I didn't have classes at school. During those years I had remained good friends with Burt Green.

Burt didn't like to skin the deer, elk, moose, wild pigs, etc. that hunters brought to the plant by the hundreds each fall. In whatever spare time I had, I'd go to the plant and skin them for $3.00 each. I could skin six deer per hour, and that was real big money for a college student in the Sixties.

I received my B.A. degree in 1969, but decided I didn't want to be a high school history teacher after all. I was offered a chance to buy the business, Green's Locker Service, in Elk Grove. Without a dime to call my own after nine years of earning only enough money to be able to stay in school, Burt and I worked out a deal and I bought the business.

After four years, I had expanded the business to the point that I would either have to compromise my standards to keep up with demand, or go into debt for the rest of my life and build a large plant. I sold, went to real estate school, and have been a real estate broker ever since.

Over the years, my knowledge of every facet of the meat business has served my friends and family well.

In 1968, I was issued a "Lifetime Credential to Teach Meat Cutting to Adult Classes" by the State of California. The original, now lost, was signed by Ronald Reagan. I got a replacement about a year ago, called a "Standard Designated Subjects Teaching Credential," which means I can teach any subject to adult classes that I've done for more than two years. It impressed a couple of teachers who happened to be in my office a few weeks ago. It doesn't mean zip to me, but they were awed to be in my august presence.

I hope you will benefit from greatly from what you might learn in this publication. I've tried to make it very easy follow along. The only thing you can really do wrong is to do nothing. One of the beautiful things about working with meat that has always appealed to me is that I could always eat my mistakes; or mis-*steaks*, as I prefer to think of them.

Enjoy!

# Contents

# Introduction

This is not a cookbook, nor is it a complete work on the subject of Beef.

A year and a half ago, some good friends, after a meal at our house, offered to put up a web site showing just a few simple things about meat. From all the emailed thank-you notes and additional questions I've received in response to that bit of information, available at www.meatbasics101.com, I was encouraged to offer more.

The purpose of this publication is to help you, the family meat buyer, understand what you're buying in the meat department by learning some of the basics. The data presented here is practical and applicable. It is intended to help you save time, money, and a great deal of frustration.

I've tried to make it easy to follow along and simple enough that anyone can enjoy learning about it and benefiting, if only by an increased awareness of the subject.

With just some of the information, illustrations and data you'll find in the following pages, you can immediately start saving on your grocery bill.

More important, knowing and understanding what you're buying will enable you to have better beef for your buck.

If you're of a squeamish nature, this book may not suit you. Even though we rarely think about it, virtually every plant, animal and human being on earth, if they are to survive at all, must consume other things that were alive. We all wish that weren't the case, of course. Take that up with the Maker when you meet Him, if you like.

Anything and everything that we can eat was once alive: turnips, fish, carrots, lettuce, cows, peanuts, sheep, chicken or cauliflower—all were alive. Each living thing thrives when well cared for; each gets sick, withers and dies with no care or mistreatment. I've raised almost every kind of farm animal from birth and I've grown most every kind of vegetable. I wouldn't be able to tell you with any certainty at all that a cow is more alive or has more feeling than a carrot; a pig more alive than a cauliflower, or if a fish is more alive or has more feeling than an elm tree.

In all of modern man's 100,000 year history, people have eaten meat whenever and however they could get it. Only in recent times have we commoners had the luxury of time and food in enough quantity to be able reflect upon the fairness of the universe.

A very small percentage of populations are sad, sadistic individuals. When one is caught on tape practicing his sadism in a slaughterhouse, the sensationalism creates an outrage. The fact is that in this country, with rare exception, animals to be used for meat die as humanely as is possible. Cruelly treated or panic-stricken animals make poor meat. That would cut into profits. If for no other reason than the bottom line, overall, I think those in that business do a pretty decent job. Almost 300,000,000 Americans consume meat products almost every day.

It was over fifty years ago that I got a part-time job as a clean-up boy in a meat market. After I graduated from high school, I began my formal, according to the Meat Cutters Union, two-year apprenticeship. Thirteen years later I left the meat business to go into the real estate business, which I've been doing since then. I've continued to observe the evolving meat business, and have learned to be, by the acclaim of family and friends, a pretty fair "chef." Of course, the more any cook knows about what they're cooking, the better "chef" they can become.

Many years ago I saw a customer seriously ask a meat cutter that I was working alongside where pork and veal came from. He seriously told her, "The right side of a calf is veal, and the left side of the calf is pork. Veal only comes the right side of a calf." She seriously believed him.

If that were an isolated incident, it would be funny. From the questions I get from other shoppers when I'm buying meat at a meat counter, or from friends, I continue to be surprised at how little knowledge and how much misinformation meat shoppers are armed with. (If you happen to be the dear lady above, the whole calf is veal; the whole pig is pork.)

Where do we learn about what most of us consume every day? Mom and dad didn't know, and their parents didn't know or they would have taught them. The subject isn't taught in school. What most people think they know about meat is usually wrong. The sellers of meats and their advertisers and marketers tell us everything they think we need to know in their ads and promotions. That should be enough, right? The only thing the meat sellers are going to teach us is whatever serves their purpose first—not what serves their customers' purposes.

## Butcher, Meat Cutter or Meat Clerk?

I should clarify the difference between a "butcher" and a "meat cutter." Today, most people who work in most meat markets are neither. Most chain store supermarkets today receive the main cuts and primals (primary sections of the beef) in vacuum-sealed packages. All that remains to be done is to open the package, slice the steaks and roasts, re-grind the coarsely ground beef, and package the cuts for the counter. Some meat departments today receive the individual steaks, roasts and all other cuts already individually packaged and ready for the counter. A clerk doesn't even have to open the package, but simply re-stock as needed.

Before the days of refrigeration, there was only the "butcher." One of the old-timers who taught me the trade had been a butcher in the late

1800's, and was still a meat cutter into the late 1950's. He told me about how he'd hitch his horse up to his wagon at 3 A.M., butcher and skin a steer, take it to his butcher shop and cut it up. He'd then load the meat on his meat wagon and begin his meat-pedaling route. His customers would select what they wanted to cook that day from his wagon, pay him, and he'd be on to the next customer. When he'd sold everything on the wagon, he'd return to the shop, make bologna or sausages, corned beef, etc., and generally end the day when the entire steer, and/or hogs and/or sheep were sold and utilized.

With the advent of refrigeration, the meat wagon was a thing of the past. Specialization followed, and with the beginnings of trade unions, "butchers" slaughtered the animals, "skinners" skinned them, "meat cutters" cut them up, and "sausage makers" made sausage. I was never a butcher, and very few meat cutters even at that time were ever "butchers." The name is still generally used when referring to anyone working behind a meat counter.

I was amused last week when I was looking for a boneless Cross Rib Roast at one of the national chain supermarkets. I asked the meat cutter who was restocking the counter if he would be putting more out. He told me, "No, we're all out, but why not get a Sirloin Tip Roast, it's the same thing." Either the poor fellow, also known as a "meat specialist," really didn't know the difference between a Cross Rib and a Sirloin Tip, or he was playing with me.

In this day of meat departments receiving pre-packaged almost everything, he might well not have known the difference; or even that the Cross Rib comes from the front quarter and the Sirloin Tip comes from the hindquarter of the beef.

Yesterday I bought four pieces of pork belly[1] at a local market. The young meat cutter who waited on me asked what I was going to do

---

[1] Bacon is made from "Pork Belly."

with it as the total weight was over sixteen pounds. I told him I was going to cure it for about a week, smoke it in my little smoke house, and have some great bacon. He asked with a surprised look, "Is that where bacon comes from?" I assured him it was. "But what about the bones?" "I'll just slide those out and we'll have spare-ribs for dinner tonight," I told him. "Are those spare-ribs?" he asked.

What I have tried to accomplish here is to take most of the mystery out where different cuts of beef come from, what to do with it, and how to make the most out of the dollars you spend on meat.

This book deals only with the subject of beef, and I've tried to show and tell not virtually everything that I could, but only in enough detail and photos to make it as useful as possible by anyone who buys meat today from their local supermarket or meat market. While I have made some historical references, it's what's in the counter today that I've concentrated on helping you with.

In 2007, in the U.S., per capita, we consumed about 220 pounds of all meats, including fish and shell fish. That means that for every man, woman and child in the U.S., we consumed 9.6 ounces of meat of all kinds per day.

Statistically, we had a per capita consumption of:

| Type of meat | Pounds consumed in 1975 | Pounds consumed in 2007 |
|---|---|---|
| Beef | 85 | 66 |
| Pork | 43 | 51 |
| Lamb | 2 | 1 |
| Chicken | 39 | 87 |
| Turkey | 7 | 17 |
| Veal | 2 | 1 |
| Fish and Shellfish | 47 | 69 |

We used 178 pounds per capita in the US in 1975, and 222 pounds per capita in 2007.

We rank third among the countries of the world, per capita, in our consumption of beef and veal, seventeenth in our consumption of pork, and second in our consumption of poultry.

Politics, special interests and emotions aside, the worldwide demand for meat of all kinds has increased by 50% over the last sixty years. It seems our compassion for the animals specifically raised to feed people might be shared with a little compassion for the billion or so starving people in the world. To think that if we eat less meat the grain that fed the animals would go to the starving may be naive. From what I've observed, it goes to warlords, politicians and other gangsters, to be sold to the highest bidder.

Perhaps we should export and teach the sustainable farming technology already fully developed, even for barren deserts, instead of sending grain, and stop buying the idea that there's a shortage of farmland. There isn't.

# Becoming More Aware

**W**e've all seen the charts of a side of beef, a side of pork, lamb, etc., showing where the various cuts come from. I've yet to find anyone who actually understood them well enough for one to be useful. I've included a simple one of those here, but what makes sense to you is what you see in the meat counter today. That is something you can use and work with.

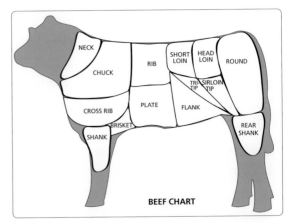

BEEF CHART

Practices and operating procedures in the meat business have changed dramatically over the last thirty-five years, much like they have in every other field. Today very little beef is delivered from the slaughterhouse to markets in quarters, that is, by the hindquarter and by the front quarter.

Today, the various primals (primary sections of the beef) arrive at the markets in shrink-wrapped, plastic packages inside cardboard boxes. The beef is broken down into the various primals at the "meat processing plant," which may be in Washington, Iowa, Kansas or Texas. Political correctness has apparently deemed the word, "slaughterhouse," to be unacceptable, so we now call it the "processing plant." Unfortunately, the word "processing" has any number of meanings.

That the whole subject of meat is little understood by most people is obvious by a quick walk down any meat counter in any supermarket.

I'm often amazed to see some cut of meat labeled "seasoned," "marinated" or "oven ready" for sale at up to $2.00 per pound more than exactly the same cut, but without the dime's worth of seasoning in making it "oven ready." Anyone could accomplish exactly the same effect by using the seasonings they probably have at home, yet they'll pay $3.00 to $6.00 more for that "seasoned," three-pound piece of meat without really giving it any thought.

Sometimes a marinated oven-ready cut of meat is worth the price to us because of time, convenience, or a special flavor we love but can't quite duplicate. When we know we have more choices, know exactly what we're doing and why were doing it, we have the good feeling of self-confidence. When we don't know what our options are, don't really understand what we're buying, we feel uneasy and uncertain. I don't like feeling that I don't have a choice, or that I don't really know what I'm buying, no matter what the product happens to be. I don't think anyone else does either. We don't tolerate that "don't know" feeling when we're buying a TV or a toaster, yet most people tolerate it one to three times every day in the wheat, meat, vegetables or fruit we consume.

I certainly don't advocate doing anything to excess, including meat consumption. I do advocate knowing exactly what it is that composes our diet.

Change occurs more and more quickly in every field. The marketing of meat is no exception. Fierce competition keeps the profit margin in the meat department of a supermarket extremely small. Very few industries operate on such narrow margins. Forty-five years ago, a meat department manager pointed out to me that the difference between our showing a profit or a loss for a three-month period amounted to one penny per package of meat sold. For example if we got $2.19, for a given package of meat, we made a profit. If we sold the same package for $2.18, we had a loss for that quarter of the year. Prices have changed since then, but the margins and percentages have not.

How long has it been since you've seen a stand-alone meat market? If you're under seventy-five, you probably haven't. Unless it's a specialty meat market, within a specialty grocery store, "butcher shops" are all but a historical footnote. I was very lucky to happen on one such specialty meat market, "Alexander's Prime Meats" within Howie's Ranch Market, in San Gabriel, CA. We were very graciously welcomed into their walk-in refrigerator to take photos of a USDA Prime front quarter and the USDA Prime hindquarter for this book. (And it was a pleasure to see magnificent cuts of beautifully aged USDA Prime beef, at fair prices, in a meat counter again!)

Meat departments in chain grocery stores are extremely competitive. Grocery store management knows that people will ordinarily do most of their grocery shopping in the store where they buy their meat. Grocery stores depend on people buying the items with higher profit margins, and generally use the meat department to draw customers. They don't generally expect their meat department to make much money, if any at all. Probably the first thing on the first page of any grocery store advertisement you've ever seen is the meat specials for the week. A can of beans or a box of dish soap isn't perishable—meat is. If meat isn't well handled, kept refrigerated, well marketed and sold in a timely fashion, it can become a total loss.

The weight of the bones alone on a side of beef is roughly 20% of the total weight. When the primal cuts are de-boned and the excess external fat is removed before being shrink wrapped, roughly another 10-15% of the weight is removed. Shipping costs are reduced by roughly 30% in packaging and shipping boneless beef, trimmed of most of its fat, rather than shipping the full quarter of beef.

We find recipes for things like a Rump Roast, a full Round Steak, a Round Bone Roast, etc., yet we haven't seen one of those in a meat market for many years. The bones in those cuts are heavy and expensive to ship.

Rump Roasts used to contain a portion of the hip joint and pelvic bone. It was the beginning of the full Round, and contained the uppermost end of the three main muscles that compose the Round. The bone-in Rump Roast contained that portion of the Top Round— what we today call "London Broil," as well a portion of the Bottom Round and a portion of the Eye of Round. Today, Rump Roast is only the boneless first cut of the Bottom Round.

*The whole Bottom Round*

*Cutting a Rump Roast off the whole Bottom Round*

We have only Cross Rib Roasts and the Cross Rib by another name, Shoulder Clod Roast, rather than the Round Bone Roasts of yesteryear. It's getting harder to find even a Chuck Roast that isn't boneless.

*Boneless Rump*

It seems odd that you can usually buy a Boneless Eye of Rib for about $1.00 less per pound than a Bone-in Standing Rib of the same grade. This USDA Choice Bone-in Beef Rib Roast was purchased for $5.99 per pound.

*Choice Rib Roast*

In the same counter, on the same day, you could purchase a USDA Choice Boneless Rib Eye for $4.99 per pound. That means, roughly, that if you buy the bone-in roast, you're paying an additional $8.00 just for the three rib bones in an eight-pound Standing Rib Roast. Those three bones, with the meat removed, will weigh around nine ounces, meaning you're paying roughly $15.00 per pound for the bare bones.

*Rib bones*

For example, if an eight-pound Bone-in Standing Rib Roast, USDA Choice grade, is available at $5.99 per pound, it will cost a total of $47.92. A whole Boneless Rib Eye, USDA Choice grade, at $4.99 per pound will cost $39.92, for the same eight pounds. Other than the traditional appearance of the roast before carving, there's no difference at all in the meat.

Marketing, creativity, advertising and promotional activities of all kinds are meant to increase sales and profits in any business. That is no less true in the meat business. The names of cuts of meat are changed to sound more exotic; recipes are printed out and freely available to accompany some of the different cuts of meat in the counter, displays are made to be very appetizing and appealing—all in an effort to show a profit at the end of the day.

We see and hear advertisements and promotions for undoubtedly very fine steaks and ground beef offered by specialty meat companies: "The finest beef money can buy," or some such, costing up to ten times more than what anyone could produce just as well or better right at home—with just a little understanding.

# Grades of Beef

Some years ago, before fat in the diet became the unwarranted villain it is today, all the major supermarkets carried only USDA Choice graded beef. Today some carry un-graded beef, some carry USDA Select, and some carry both Select and un-graded beef. A few supermarkets carry only USDA Choice and/or USDA Prime beef. USDA Prime graded beef generally has a higher fat content than most people want. The cost of a side or quarter of USDA Prime is usually about the same as USDA Choice, and sometimes less. The difference in the final cost of the individual cuts of meat is in the amount of fat that has to be trimmed away.

There are eight grades of beef, as designated by Graders of the United States Department of Agriculture (USDA).

After the beef has been killed, skinned, eviscerated, split into two halves and chilled overnight, the Grader, if that beef is to be graded, evaluates the carcass.

The side of beef, hanging from the rear shank, has been cut laterally with a knife—twelve ribs up from the neck, from the backbone to the brisket bone. At the top of the twelfth rib is where the separation between the front quarter and the hindquarter is made. The last rib bone, the smallest, a "floating rib," is left on the hindquarter. The eye of the rib is exposed to the grader.

After the grader has evaluated the overall shape or contour of the beef, the marbling, the fat content, the color of the fat and meat, and the animal's approximate age, he or she rolls a stamp all along the carcass which says one of the following:

- USDA Prime

- USDA Choice

- USDA Select

- USDA Standard

- USDA Commercial

- USDA Utility

- USDA Canner

- USDA Cutter

Very few supermarkets carry USDA Choice beef today. With the idea that too much animal fat was in the American diet, markets starting shifting to leaner, cheaper grades of beef in the Seventies and Eighties. Until then, nearly every major supermarket and major grocery store carried only USDA Choice beef.

I'm going to digress here for a moment and talk about what makes beef tender and flavorful—it's the fat. Beef without fat is tough, dry and flavorless. Fat alone gives beef its flavor, its moisture and its tenderness. "Marbling" is the specks of fat interspersed throughout any muscle or any "eye" of any cut of meat.

When I speak of the "eye" of any cut, I'm talking about the center or main muscle of that cut. It would not include the "tail" or distinct smaller, outer muscles. The eye of most cuts is usually the most tender, best marbled and most flavorful.

Some national chain stores advertise ungraded beef under various names to make them seem more special: "Cowboy's Pride", "Farmers' Reserve" or anything that seems to set it apart and above the USDA Select or ungraded meat they also have available. It may or may not be even as high in quality as USDA Select, yet the unique label alone automatically makes it appear more valuable.

# USDA Inspection versus USDA Grading

The grading of beef and inspection by the USDA are two different actions. Beef doesn't have to be graded at all. The USDA must inspect *all* meat that is to be sold whether it is sold to wholesale or to retail outlets. Meat to be sold to the public must bear the stamp, "Inspected by the USDA" either on the meat itself or on the packaging that contains it.

In addition, that stamp must have an identification number showing where it was inspected and passed if it is to be sold the public in any form. Selling uninspected meat in the U.S. is a serious crime, yet very often the only selling point on a package of meat is highlighted in the advertisement, "Inspected by the USDA."

## Beef Grading is Voluntary—
## Inspection by the USDA is Mandatory

Having beef graded is a voluntary action of the meat packer. If beef is graded, the meat packer must pay the Grader's wages. The Grader is an employee of the U.S. Department of Agriculture.

As grading is voluntary, meat packers usually don't want or need to pay for grading anything they know won't carry the stamp "USDA Select", "USDA Choice" or "USDA Prime." Meats that won't make one of those three grades generally aren't graded at all. As the Grader doesn't grade them, a grade stamp isn't rolled onto the beef. Those that aren't graded are called "no rolls." The grades below Standard are generally used for making a large variety of beef and beef-based products, including lunch meats, sausages, salamis, canned soups and canned meats of all kinds.

Cut-rate grocery stores and meat markets generally buy USDA Standard or below, whether it's been graded and rolled, or not officially graded at all. The lower grades of beef have less fat and are generally comparatively tough when cooked in traditional American and

European ways. Because of variations in cooking customs, practices and recipes, some ethnics and people on special diets require no fat at all in their beef. These grades are ideal for the many different ways of preparing fatless beef, for making ground beef, stews, and for long, slow cooking methods of all kinds.

Without "USDA" in front of a grade, any description such as "Choice", "Prime", "Select", "Ranchers Pride", " Selected" or other such words, have no real or standardized meaning at all. Using the word "Prime" or "Choice" alone is not a misrepresentation. Anyone could call anything by any word. Only a Department of Agriculture Grader can perform the labeling of meat as "USDA Choice", "USDA Select" or whatever the grade might be. If a market isn't advertising and labeling their beef USDA Prime, USDA Choice or USDA Select, it is something less.

A number of markets in our neighborhood don't advertise any grade at all. Their beef usually looks like it would grade Standard had it been graded. You may not want to buy one of those steaks for grilling or broiling, but certainly they have other uses. I buy the lower grades of beef, usually a chuck roast, for making our ground beef, stews and soups, or for mixing with pork shoulder butts for some of the various sausages and salamis I make at home.

One could call USDA Standard graded beef "Prime", "Choice" or "Select" without consequence. The line is crossed and it becomes a Federal offense to label it, advertise it, or sell it as "USDA Choice" etc., if it hasn't been graded as such by the USDA.

## What Grade of Beef Do I Want?

To begin with, you must decide what quality of beef you want to use. Whether you intend to grill or broil steaks, put a roast in the crock-pot to cook all day, or grind a roast into hamburger gives you the answer.

If you're going to buy meat for steaks, you probably want USDA Choice. USDA Prime is hard to find and expensive, and generally contains more fat and marbling than most of us want to consume on a regular basis.

If you're going to grind your own ground beef, USDA Select, USDA Standard, or no roll (un-graded) may serve nicely.

If you're going to put a roast in the crock-pot in the morning and let it cook all day, USDA Select or below is all you may want. It's going to be tender cooked that way and the fat content is less.

There are only two stores in our neighborhood that carry USDA Choice beef. For steaks and special roasts, I buy only USDA Choice primal cuts. I normally will want to age the whole primal in our second refrigerator for at least ten days, usually about twenty days, before cutting them into steaks or roasts. Costco usually has whole Boneless Beef Ribs, whole New York Strips, whole Sirloin Tips, etc., in the counter at a very fair price. I'll sometimes buy a USDA Choice Sirloin Tip, which is as pure lean as any cut on the beef, to mix with fatter chuck roasts of a lesser grade. That combination can produce a ground beef that is very lean yet has enough fat to give it a very good flavor. The marbling and fat content of USDA Choice beef isn't usually wanted or needed for slow cooking a roast in the crock-pot, cutting up into cubes for stews or soups, or for making ground beef.

Ground alone, the trimmings from USDA Choice beef are generally going to be too fat for ground beef. Chuck Roasts, usually boneless, and Shoulder Clods (Cross Rib) are frequently on sale at one or another of the supermarkets that carries USDA Select, and even some markets that sell ungraded beef. Those grades are better suited for slow cooking, for soups and stews, or for any other use that requires minimal fat and marbling.

We see advertising promoting "free range, grass fed, all natural" or "organic" beef. The prices per pound of this meat can be staggering.

It doesn't cost much to let a steer graze right up until it's time to go to market, although more labor is involved in moving the herds from pasture to pasture. It costs a great deal to put the same steer in a feedlot and give it all the corn and grain it wants for ninety days. I've had "grass fed" beef several times and to this day I've had none that was tender, tasted "good" to me, or even had a flavor that I could enjoy.

We were recently gifted with some very expensive steaks that were touted as "organic, free range," and several other adjectives. They were indeed beautiful; almost no fat, no marbling, and the fat, what there was of it, was yellowish. Grain-fed beef has white fat. The fat of grass-fed beef is yellow and has a very different flavor. Most people find it distasteful. My wife and I felt very badly that this expensive present of steaks could simply not be chewed, nor was the flavor one that we could appreciate. I made the remainder into a very good smoked jerky and the gift was very much appreciated in that form. Meat suitable for jerky, however, could be bought for about 10% of what was paid for those steaks.

When I owned what was then Green's Locker Service, in Elk Grove, CA, once or twice each year some fellow would have four or five of his cattle slaughtered at his ranch. As it's very illegal to sell uninspected meat, he would sell a live steer to two different people with the understanding it was now their live animal. They paid the butcher who would butcher the beef in the field and bring the carcass to the Locker plant. I would cut, wrap and freeze it to their specifications, with each of the two halves going separately to the two owners. Out of the eight or ten customers who had bought the four or five cattle, invariably I had eight or ten unhappy customers.

They would come to see me, sometimes in groups, sometimes individually, to find out what had happened. "The meat was tough," "it had a bad flavor," etc. They demanded to know what I had done to their free range, grass fed, unpolluted, organic beef that they had paid between 50% and 250% more than what they could have bought the finest grain fed, USDA Choice beef for.

I always lost almost an hour of "show and tell," giving them an education in beef buying. Of course it made them furious at the fellow who sold them the cattle, and of course that fellow would never send his suckers to me again, knowing that I would educate them if they asked me. But, as P.T. Barnum would have known, I had a whole new crop of them every now and then from some other character.

I've read something to the effect that "grass-fed organic beef isn't graded because it is of such a different standard that it doesn't fit within the usual way of grading beef." Some portion of the population prefers it to grain-fed beef.

Last week I received the following email from a friend who was considering buying a live animal to be processed for meat.

*Hi Lee, I have an acquaintance that has raised a cow on grains and alfalfa. Her husband and she wish to have it slaughtered and have asked me if I would like to buy half of the cow. I know absolutely nothing about this. They have someone that would slaughter the cow, but he is not a meat cutter. They are meeting with a local cutter to see what he has to say. She believes he charges about $1.00 per pound to cut and package the meat. I told her that before we would take them up on this possible offer I would need to do some research. I will be searching the Internet for data this week. But, I thought I would check with you as well, in view of your experience in this area. Do you have any leads or recommendations on how one could proceed with this? I am intrigued by the idea of obtaining excellent meat from a good source, like this. What are your thoughts?*
*– Beth*

I wrote back:

*Hi Beth, my questions would include:*

1. *What breed is the animal? Angus, Hereford, Charolais, Brahma crossbreed, Guernsey, Jersey, Ayrshire, Holstein, or?*

2.    *How old is it?*

3.    *Is it a heifer or a steer? Or, heaven forbid, still a bull?*

4.    *How long was it fed on grain? Was it penned up for the last ninety days and given all the grain it would eat? Or is it free range in the alfalfa field and given a couple of pounds of grain every other day or so?*

5.    *How much per pound. do they want for it? Is that the live (on-the-hoof) weight or the carcass-hanging weight after it's slaughtered?*

6.    *Where is it going to be slaughtered?*

7.    *Where would the carcass be taken to cool after slaughter?*

8.    *How long could you leave it there to age before it's processed?*

9.    *Would the meat cutter cut it to your exact specifications while you watched?*

10.    *Would he double-wrap each package in plastic wrap, prior to the final wrap in butcher paper?*

11.    *Would he then quick-freeze it at −10 to −20 degrees °F?*

12.    *Check the price of "beef, live weight" on the internet or in a newspaper that has commodity prices. The last time I looked, which was months ago, it was about $1.08 per pound on the hoof.*

*On the breeds under 1) above, you'll lose between 45% and 55% of the live weight in turning it into four quarters hanging on the hook even before it's cut up. Then, if it's as fat as it has to be in order to have good beef, you'll lose another 40%, if you have it all boneless and well trimmed of fat. The on-the-hoof, 1,000-pound, high-quality steer will become about 330 pounds of boneless, packaged meat. If it's one of the dairy breeds listed above, or if it isn't very fat, you'll do a bit better percentage wise, but the quality of the meat won't be nearly as good. (They use those for processed meats of all kinds and in canned products.)*

*So, if it is a high quality beef animal, and if it weighs 1,000 pounds on the hoof, and if you pay $1.08 per pound live weight, your cost will be $3.27*

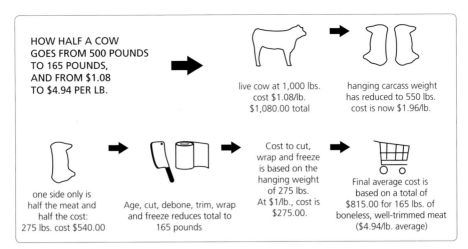

HOW HALF A COW
GOES FROM 500 POUNDS
TO 165 POUNDS,
AND FROM $1.08
TO $4.94 PER LB.

live cow at 1,000 lbs.
cost $1.08/lb.
$1,080.00 total

hanging carcass weight
has reduced to 550 lbs.
cost is now $1.96/lb.

one side only is
half the meat and
half the cost:
275 lbs. cost $540.00

Age, cut, debone, trim, wrap
and freeze reduces total to
165 pounds

Cost to cut,
wrap and freeze
is based on the
hanging weight
of 275 lbs.
At $1/lb., cost is
$275.00.

Final average cost is
based on a total of
$815.00 for 165 lbs. of
boneless, well-trimmed meat
($4.94/lb. average)

*per pound after it's cut, wrapped and frozen, if it's cut, wrapped and frozen for free. If it costs another $1.00 a pound for that[1], it will be charged on the hanging weight.*

*If the half of the 550-pound whole carcass weighs 275 pounds, that's another $275 to be factored in, giving you 550 pounds of whole beef, hanging weight, which costs $1,080 (the 1,000-pound live steer at $1.08 per pound), 275 pounds of a half beef, hanging weight costs $540, plus $275 to get it cut wrapped and frozen, and hopefully aged for ten days to two weeks, giving you a total of $815 for your 165 pounds of packaged, boneless meat. That equates to $4.94 per pound for every pound and every cut—hamburger, flank steak, bottom round, etc. And you won't really know if it's good until you cook some of it, way after it's too late to turn back.*

*As to "custom farm kill," the fellow drives up in a pick-up with a hoist, kills the animal, hoists it up, eviscerates it, skins it, and takes it wherever requested. There it's split and quartered, the quarters rolled into a chilling room overnight (because the body heat steams tremendously in the cooler, creating lots of moisture condensation), and from there into a walk-in cooler, where it should hang for the next ten to fourteen days, or more.*

*No matter the butcher, I've never seen a farm-killed animal that didn't have intestinal matter around the shanks—at the very least. You, the meat cutter, try to take it all off, but there's just no way you ever get it all. Winds*

---

[1] In 1973, I got eight cents per pound for a truly first class job.

*up flavoring the hamburger, you see. I always tried my best to get people to take their animals to the slaughterhouse, one mile away from my plant, where it would be killed under the strictest sanitary standards, under the watch of a USDA meat inspector.*

*And I always had to explain to some fellow's "good friends" why the "range free, pure organic" meat they had bought from their friendly little farmer friend—at twice the price they'd have wound up paying at a chain store for really good beef—wasn't anything like they were used to, nor what they expected. There may have been some exception, but I don't remember one friendly little organic farmer selling anyone meat that way for a second time. Mostly, the buyers wanted to do bodily harm to the little bastard.*

*Me? Wouldn't do it on a bet. No matter how good a beef looks on the hoof, until you cut into it a few weeks later, you just don't know. That's why I buy whole boneless USDA Select shoulder chucks or very large chuck roasts for a lot of things—hamburger, salami, corned beef, pastrami, a roast or two, and sometimes even a really good couple of steaks—for about $2.50 a pound; whole USDA Choice Ribs or New York Strips for about $4.50–5.00 a pound, and age them, or USDA Select top round, Sirloin Tip, or some such, for about $1.99 a pound when we need or want very lean beef for some reason. Overall, you'd be paying just about double for your meat.*

*How can that be the case? Two reasons:*

1. *The economy of volume, and*
2. *The little guys don't get the farm subsidies that the big guys get. (That's a whole other book that somebody should write.)*

*See, Beth, you never want to ask a guy with Irish genes a one-answer question. Not unless you're ready to hear the long version of the story of creation, you don't.*

— Lee

# Organic Beef

As in beef grading, without the USDA in front of "Organic" on the label, it means nothing at all.

The standards for the USDA Certification of Organic Beef were first published in 2002. They are rigid and expensive to comply with relative to the usual methods that have been in practice for one hundred years or more. Until production catches up with demand by more producers switching to organic methods, the price of organic meats will remain relatively high.

There's no standard set for "natural," "naturally grown," or any trade name. Such words could mean anything. If you pay more because it has such a label, you're being taken advantage of.

USDA Certified Organic means:

> *"Organic food is produced using sustainable agricultural production practices. Not permitted are most conventional pesticides; fertilizers made with synthetic ingredients, or sewage sludge; bioengineering; or ionizing radiation. Organic meat, poultry eggs, and dairy products come from animals that are given no antibiotics or growth hormones."*
> – excerpted from www.usda.gov

"USDA Prime Beef" has met very strict requirements, and you know it is the best beef money can buy. USDA Organic beef isn't graded. Any particular beef might have graded Prime or Choice, but we don't know, nor do we have any way of knowing, how it might have graded. As far as the quality of the beef is concerned, you're on your own.

It's difficult and expensive for beef producers to attain certification, and it's costly to produce good beef. Good beef, the kind we're used to, can't be fed on grass alone. Cattle graze because they're looking for food. If they have all they want and are getting all the nutrients their bodies need, they're perfectly content to stay in one place. Organically raised cattle only have to have access to open areas—they don't have to go there.

For beef to be what we expect it to be, it must be fed all the good grain and rich hay it will eat. That costs money. If someone can convince us to pay twice as much for beef that cost half as much to produce, so much the better—for them. I'll have a nice salad and some sautéed vegetables rather than tough, flavorless beef any time.

We hear about growth hormones in the feed of mass-produced cattle, but how many of us know exactly what that means? I use loads of growth hormones in my purely organic gardens—they are a natural part of kelp meal, which also contains over seventy trace minerals. What kind of "growth hormones" are fed to the cattle? And do we really know what, if any, affect it might have on those who eat it? I'm very cautious about accepting "scientific research." I want to know who did it, which company paid for the research, and all the details of that "research." We get a news blip something on the order of, "Growth hormones found to be..." or some such, and we're suddenly afraid. It seems to me that if there were any such proven links to any negative effects, we'd all know about it.

Growing our own meat isn't possible for most of us anymore. If I could raise my own beef, I would certainly use whatever antibiotics were needed to keep it healthy, I'd feed it nothing but organically grown hay and grain, and I wouldn't let it run around in a large pasture for the last ninety days of its life.

Personally, I'd like to know that the meat products I use were in fact given antibiotics. I'd rather not think of some sick steer naturally recovering from some disease that should have been avoided in the first place winding up on my plate.

I write articles, speak to groups about organic gardening, and generally promote the boycott of chemical pesticides and fertilizers in favor of organic methods whenever and wherever I can. I've been growing virtually all of our vegetables purely organically for well over twenty years. I'm rabidly against the use of chemicals in the growing of any fruit, grain or vegetables. We know all about that area of agriculture and we have choices that we can clearly make with great confidence. None of what we grow, no matter how hard we try, is 100% organic. Our air is a mess, our water worse. The microscopic airborne debris that lands on our soil and the impossible-to-remove chemical residues in our water makes perfection impossible to achieve in any garden. The best we can do is to not add to the chemical soup we're immersed in and hope that's good enough.

Whether to buy all or some of your beef from USDA Certified growers is a personal choice, of course. As in anything else, before making a choice, we need all the information we can get. Once you know that, you can move cautiously ahead. If it is USDA Certified Organic, was the animal well fed? Of course the feed had to be organically grown, but was it honestly fattened up to the degree that the meat is tender and flavorful? In my experience, most people who want no fat at all buy chicken breasts or white fish. They don't eat hamburgers or thick juicy steaks. When most of us want beef, we want beef we can eat with gusto. USDA Certified Organic isn't a certification that the meat is tender, flavorful, extremely fat or extremely lean; it only means it was grown under the strict standards required for organic certification. USDA Organic Certification isn't a license to sell poor quality, fatless, flavorless beef. It can and should be well fed and well cared for, and if that is properly done, its quality should be at least equal to the quality that most of us have become used to over a lifetime.

While I am personally 100% anti-chemical in food production, I am also 100% against betrayal of the public's trust by profiting from their lack of information and knowledge. When and if USDA Choice or

Select quality, USDA Organic Beef primal sections are available to the public at fair prices, I'll be first in line.

# Sex in the Feedlot

As with all life forms, the differences between male and female cattle are numerous and significant—especially when it comes to the beef you buy.

## The Bull

A steer was born a bull but was castrated when it was a few days old. Left to grow up to be a bull, it would grow a large neck and shoulders have virtually no body fat, no marbling, and meat so tough that it's impossible to chew unless it's ground up. Generally the only use of bull meat is to add it to fat beef trimmings for ground beef. Ground beef is made redder and leaner with the addition of bull meat.

In the days when we broke down full quarters of beef in the meat department of the supermarket, we often also boned out quarters of bulls. The only purpose was to make the hamburger redder and leaner. USDA Choice beef trimmings simply contain too much fat to make anything like a lean ground beef. The more bull meat that was added, the leaner the ground beef. How much bull meat got added made the difference between "Ground Round", "Ground Chuck," and "Hamburger." In by-gone days it was never called ground beef, only "Hamburger", "Ground Round" or "Ground Chuck." (The two terms, "hamburger" and "ground beef" may be used interchangeably throughout this writing and have exactly the same meaning.)

Today it's all "ground beef" that we find in the meat counters. It's labeled, "Not more than 22% fat," or "ground beef, not more than 10% fat," or whatever the case might be. I think that's a more honest label. In fact, we never ground only Chuck for the "Ground Chuck," and we never ground only Round for the "Ground Round." It was only a question of how much bull had to be added to make the fatter trimmings lean enough to call "Ground Chuck" or "Ground Round." Truth-in-labeling laws have precluded those labels and we now have such things as "80% lean ground beef." There's still a lot of bull involved, I think.

Every once in a while, while one of us in a retail market was boning out a quarter of bull, a customer would want to buy some of that rich red meat with absolutely no fat on it. Usually, when we explained it was bull meat and that there was no way to make it tender enough to eat except by grinding it, they believed us. Now and then someone just knew we were lying and absolutely insisted we cut him or her some steaks or a roast from that beautiful red meat with no fat on it. When we had no choice, we did, knowing that we would never see that customer again. You simply can't chew bull meat cooked in the form of a steak or roast.

## The Heifer

A heifer is the female beef before having a calf. If a heifer is to be used for milk production, it is bred, has a calf, and is thereafter a milk cow. Among the primary breeds of cattle used for milk production are Holstein, Guernsey, Jersey, and Ayrshire. Breeds of cattle to be used for beef production include primarily the Angus and Hereford, usually cross-bred with a handful of other breeds.

In all breeds of cattle, the number of females exceeds the number of males that are born. In nature, fewer bulls are needed, thus fewer are born.

The meat from heifers generally has more exterior fat and less marbling. Even though a heifer is graded USDA Choice, you can often see that the muscle development isn't as full, and there's more fat outside the muscle. Because of less marbling, the meat is generally less flavorful than meat from a steer.

# The Steer

A steer is a castrated bull. A steer will generally grow a little larger and faster than a heifer. It will have less exterior fat and larger, more filled out muscles, more marbling and more flavor. Being aware of that, if you practice a bit, you'll be able to spot the difference when looking at steaks or roasts in the meat counter—if there is both heifer and steer in the counter to compare.

The usual birth weight of a calf from a beef breed is around eighty pounds. After four to five months, the calf will weigh roughly 400 pounds when it's weaned. Up until that age, calves to be used for veal aren't fed grass, grain or hay, which would darken the meat. The calf is fed only milk, which keeps the meat very light in color, bland in flavor, and typically quite tender. When the calves start eating grass, hay and grain, the meat darkens. At six to twelve months, the meat is generally the color of beef, and is called "Baby Beef." As it will generally have neither the tenderness of veal nor the full flavor of mature beef, Baby Beef is rarely promoted.

The beef we're used to seeing in the markets is typically taken when the animal was eighteen to twenty-four months old, and weighed in the neighborhood of 1,000 pounds.

**BEEF SECRETS straight from the BUTCHER**   *Lee O'Hara*

# What Becomes of That Thousand-Pound Steer?

**W**henever I sold a "half" or a "side of beef" to a new customer, I had to carefully explain about bones and excess fat. Even though they were buying a 275-pound USDA Choice side of beef, after it was cut and wrapped they would usually get back 165–200 pounds of packaged meat, depending on how boneless they wanted the various cuts.

To those who had raised a steer for the first time, had it butchered at the local meat company, and the carcass delivered to my plant for processing, the same education was even more necessary. Cut to their specifications, wrapped and frozen, their 1000-pound steer had been reduced to 330 pounds of packaged, boneless, well-trimmed cuts of beef.

Where did the other 670 pounds go?

From that 1,000-pound steer, the hide alone weighs about 100 pounds, or about 10% of the live weight. With hide, head, hooves and interior gone, the carcass weighs about 55% of the live weight, or about 550 pounds.

That weight, in the form of the two front quarters and the two hindquarters, was what the meat company delivered to my plant. If the steer was of USDA Choice quality, and the customer wanted all boneless steaks and roasts and

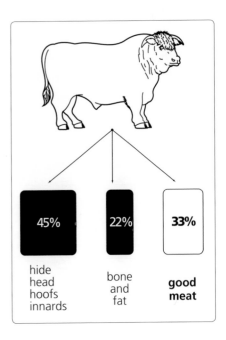

| | | |
|---|---|---|
| 45% | 22% | **33%** |
| hide head hoofs innards | bone and fat | **good meat** |

normal exterior fat trimming, 40% of the hanging carcass weight went into the waste bone and fat containers. The remaining 60% of the 550-pound carcass weight, in this case 330 pounds, was boneless and well-trimmed steaks, roasts and ground beef.

In looking at the Commodities Market price just now, I see the price of live cattle is at $99.80 per hundred pounds. As 33% of those 1,000 pounds is what's left in red meat, the cost of the meat has just tripled, making it close to $3.00 per pound on the average. With the average retail cost of beef at roughly $4.00 per pound, you can see there isn't much profit, if any, by the time one pays:

- To ship the beef to the market

- Meat cutters wages

- Refrigeration and electrical costs

- Rent for the retail space utilized

- Insurance costs, and

- All the other overhead costs related to operating a meat market.

Until about thirty-five years ago, markets received beef by the quarter. That is, in most supermarkets we would typically receive about a dozen front quarters of beef and about a dozen hindquarters. They were delivered in refrigerated trucks where they had been stacked, one on top of the other, at the most local slaughterhouse early that morning. The cattle had usually been slaughtered from one to three days earlier under the watchful eye a United States Department of Agriculture (USDA) inspector. If it was to be graded according to its quality, a USDA "Grader" graded it.

# Side of Beef

Centralization of "processing plants" has helped keep the retail costs of meat at relatively lower levels than when there were slaughterhouses near every large population center.

If the beef is to be processed in the same plant, it is broken down into primal cuts, (meaning the primary, or main sections of beef,

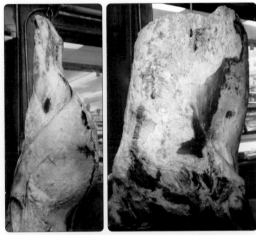

*Left: hind quarter; Right: front quarter*

such as the Chuck, Cross Rib, Round, Rib, etc.), vacuum-sealed in plastic wrap and boxed for shipment. In such a case, the plastic wrap will bear the stamp "USDA Prime", "USDA Choice", "USDA Select" or whatever the grade happens to be.

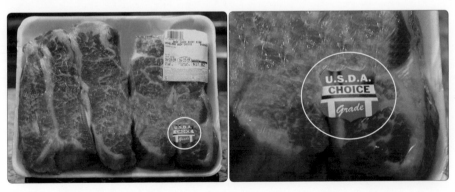

*Packaged Boneless Short Ribs—note the USDA Choice label.*

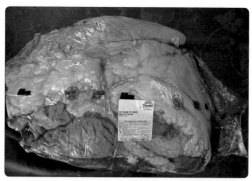

*A packaged Whole Top Round as it came from the processing plant.*

You'll also find a stamp on the plastic wrap which says, "US Inspected and passed by the Department of Agriculture, EST. 9268" (or whatever the actual establishment number of the processing plant happens to be.)

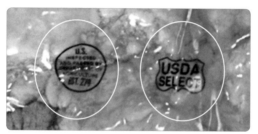

*A close view of the Whole Top Round—
note the USDA Inspected stamp on the left
and the grade stamp on the right.*

If you're in an area where you can buy beef by the "side of beef," the front and rear quarters are from the same beef—or should be. The front quarter will generally weigh roughly 10% more than the hindquarter. From a 275-pound side, the hindquarter will weigh roughly 130 pounds, and the front quarter will weigh roughly 145 pounds.

# The Front Quarter

**E**ach side of beef is cut into two quarters—the hindquarter and the front quarter. Each quarter is then divided into various major sections. These primary cuts are called "primals."

The front quarter primarily contains:

- **The Chuck** contains the Chuck Roasts, bone-in or boneless, and includes the neck.

- **The Rib** begins between the fifth and sixth rib up from the front of the beef and ends after the twelfth rib toward the hind quarter.

- **The Cross Rib**, often now called the Shoulder Clod, is immediately below the chuck.

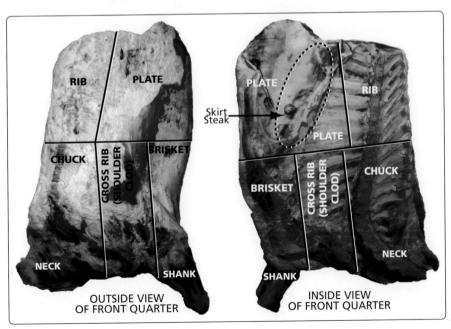

OUTSIDE VIEW OF FRONT QUARTER

INSIDE VIEW OF FRONT QUARTER

- **The Brisket** is located between the animal's front legs, just below the Cross Rib, and continues along the lower end of the Plate.

- **The Plate** begins at the lower end of the small end of the Eye of the Rib and is the same width as the Rib. The seven rib bones that compose the Rib extend down to, and end, at the breastbone, which is essentially the Brisket.

- **The Front Shank** is above the front hoof and knee. Called the Shank, this set of much-worked muscles is almost indistinguishable from the Rear Shank. Both Rear Shank and Front Shank are alike sinewy, heavily lined with membrane around the various small muscles, and contain very little fat. With the bone left in, cooked long and slow as for a soup or stew, they can be quite flavorful. Most markets don't sell as many as they might, in which case the meat, being very lean, is ground along with fatter trimmings to make ground beef.

Pictured below, on the far right, the Rib is the uppermost cut, and the top end of the front quarter where it adjoined the hindquarter.

*The approximate relative locations of various primary cuts from the front quarter (Top) Chuck, Rib; (Center) Cross Rib (Bottom) Brisket (Very bottom) Shank*

The difference between the smallest end of the Rib and the smallest end of the New York Strip (on the hindquarter), is the width of a knife blade.

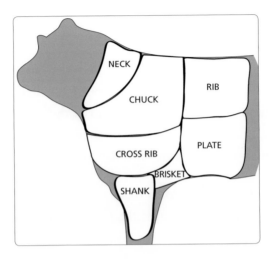

# Chuck

The Chuck is the upper shoulder, between the neck and the large end of the Rib, and above the Cross Rib, which is also known as the Shoulder Clod.

As the Chuck runs from the neck toward the Rib, the meat becomes more marbled, a little fatter, and more tender and flavorful.

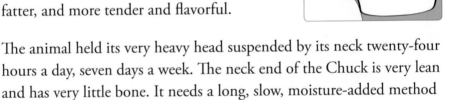

The animal held its very heavy head suspended by its neck twenty-four hours a day, seven days a week. The neck end of the Chuck is very lean and has very little bone. It needs a long, slow, moisture-added method of cooking to be chewable. It may be better used for a very lean ground beef, or for soup meat or stew.

### Chuck Roast

Usually the neck is sold as Chuck Roast, either bone-in or boneless. It's pretty easy to tell it's the neck, as the roast tends to be more rounded, has no other bone than the neck, and is very lean. It makes a good lean pot roast, or probably better still, a very lean ground beef if you have a meat grinder.

## Blade

Moving toward the Rib, the shoulder blade begins to show up. At the end nearest the neck, the shoulder blade bone is small, where it has originated at the socket containing the ball of the upper end of the shoulder bone. The shoulder blade bone then widens out, becoming the "blade," which ends in white cartilage at the large end of the Rib.

The largest end of the Rib adjoins the smallest end of the Chuck. The Chuck, for several inches, contains the flat, fanning section of the shoulder blade, and is simply called "Blade Chuck Roast."

The Blade cuts of the Chuck do contain more fat and marbling, and are therefore the most tender and best flavored portion of the Chuck.

The "Blade-cut Chuck Roast" adjoins the Rib where the Chuck is at its smallest surface area and the Rib is at its largest surface area. The "large end" of the Rib contains more fat, is better marbled and therefore more flavorful than the small end, which adjoins the Short Loin. Of course there's not much difference between a Rib Steak, bone-in or boneless, and a New York Steak, bone-in or boneless, right at that junction.

## 7-Bone Chuck Roast

Moving along the Chuck from the rib toward the neck, the next roasts are called "7-Bone Chuck Roasts."

In the following picture, no portion of the shoulder blade, including the beginning portion which resembles a "7," is present. The roast pictured therefore isn't a "7-Bone Chuck Roast," but is in fact the larger and beginning portion of the neck.

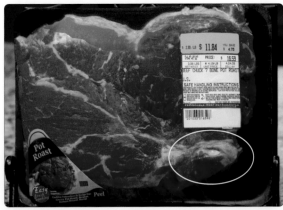

*No 7-bone present; notice the neck bone in the lower right corner.*

The white bone visible in the lower right of the photo below is actually a portion of a neck vertebra, and is more clear on the other side of the same roast.

*Same roast removed from package and turned over*

The 7-Bone Chuck Roast is so named not because it has seven bones, but because the shape of the shoulder blade more in the center of the whole chuck resembles the number 7.

49

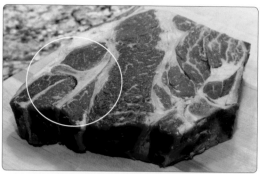

*Notice the shoulder blade bone shaped like the number 7.*

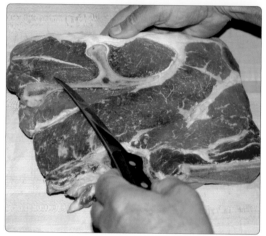

*A typical 7-Bone Roast*

The small end of the shoulder blade, near its origination, begins as a socket on the ball/knuckle bone of the upper shoulder bone. The term has come to imply only that it's the leanest of the chuck roasts.

## Cross Rib

Just below the Chuck is the "Cross Rib," or "X-Rib," or "Shoulder Clod Arm Roast."

The meat on the ribs just below the Cross Rib (it runs 'cross the rib) is thick and well marbled. This cut is often labeled "English Cut Short Ribs."

CROSS RIB

*Cross Rib Roast*

In the photo above, the Cross Rib Roast is just to the left of Boneless Short Ribs. The X-Rib is located immediately over those ribs, whether they're "Boneless" or "Bone-in English Style Short Ribs," or "Boneless Chuck Short Ribs," which may be more accurate.

*Boneless Chuck Short Ribs*

Those pictured above are in fact from the center of the Chuck primal, located just above the Eye of the Chuck, and immediately below the shoulder blade bone.

The Cross Rib is so called because it lies across the first five ribs from the front of the beef, just above the Shank, and immediately below the Chuck. Often called "Shoulder Clod," the Cross Rib is very lean, contains some very thick sinews, and isn't well marbled. If it comes from USDA Prime or Choice beef, it is generally tender enough to be oven roasted to no more than medium rare, and thinly sliced before serving. The Cross Rib has it's own unique, and generally considered to be excellent, flavor. From lesser grades of beef, it is probably better as a pot roast, or even ground for a very lean ground beef.

A thick, generally well-marbled layer of meat covers the rib bones beneath the Cross Rib, and these are most often sold as "English Style Short Ribs."

The bone removed from the Shoulder Clod, or Cross Rib, has a large knucklebone at each end, with the lower ball-or knucklebone joining the top socket of the front shank bone. The shoulder bone is the shape of bone that we think of as a very large dog bone—a fairly short round bone with a large ball at each end.

The following photo is actually a Pork Picnic Shoulder Roast, used here for the purpose of demonstration.

*Pork Picnic Shoulder*

Note that the anatomy of lamb, pork and beef are all very similar. All have similar bone and muscle structures. If it weren't for size, color and texture, it would be difficult to tell the difference in the cuts of meat taken from the comparable location of each.

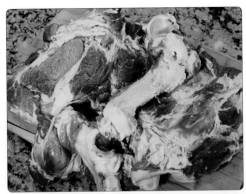

*Note the disconnected and exposed Shank bone, the Shoulder Arm bone in the center, and the exposed socket joint at the center top.*

The shoulder blade begins at the upper socket, and fans out from there, becoming the 7-Bone. A Shoulder of Beef would look very much the same.

As can be seen, the meat is very lean, but has considerable tendons, sinews and connective tissues. With the bones and most of the heavy tendons and sinews removed, on a shoulder of beef, this is the Shoulder Clod, or Cross Rib.

As the pictured shoulder is pork, the meat from this Picnic Shoulder would be more tender than would beef from the same shoulder location. I simply removed the sinews, etc., heavily seasoned it, rolled and tied it, leaving the outer skin on, and it will be excellent, either roasted in the oven or on the rotisserie.

## Rib

As you move along the Rib from large end to small, there is less marbling and less fat generally.

Most agree that the flavor of the Rib is the best there is in any cut of meat; the Filet being most tender, but less flavorful, and the New

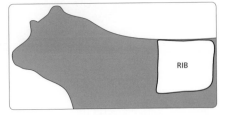

York Strip, or Loin Strip, and the Rib coming in second and third in tenderness, depending on who you ask. When I have steak, there's never a question—it's going to be from the Rib, preferably the large end. Call the boneless Rib Steak a "Spencer", "Delmonico", "Rib Eye", "Boneless Rib Eye", "Boneless Rib Steak" etc., whatever you wish; if I don't feel like I'm being gouged because of a sexy label, it's what I'll have.

## Brisket & Plate

As the Brisket moves down the side of the beef from between the front legs, toward the hindquarter, it becomes leaner.

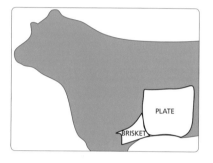

Higher up, toward the Rib, the equivalent of pork belly or side pork on a pig, the Plate is sometimes cured and smoked for "Beef Bacon."

At the bottom of the Plate lies the Brisket. At that point, for several inches above the center of the breastbone, lies the "Plate of the Brisket," or "Brisket Plate." The Brisket Plate is a thick piece of very lean, un-marbled layer of meat over the breastbone, with a thick layer of external fat. This is the cut that is most often cured for corned beef, yet it makes very dry, less tasty corned beef.

*A Brisket*

 In the photo above, the Point of the Brisket is on the left. As it moves to the right in the photo, it has become very lean, and is called the "Plate," or "Flat Plate."

Large pockets of fat can be easily removed from the Point of the Brisket, but it still contains a great deal of marbling and fat, making it superior in flavor for any use, provided it is cooked with some long, slow method, in order to tenderize it.

*Removing a pocket of fat from the Point of the Brisket*

If you have a use for both the Point and the Plate, you might want to buy a whole Brisket. It's easy to tell where the Plate should be separated from the Point.

*Cutting the Point from the Plate on a Brisket*

### Skirt Steak

A membrane separates the chest cavity and the stomach cavity of mammals. We call that membrane the diaphragm. The muscle that holds the diaphragm in place and attaches it to the inner walls of the beef is what we call Skirt Steak.

## Corned Beef

The word "corned" as in "corned beef" has nothing to do with what we think of today as corn. The Corn Laws were a series of laws, beginning in 1436 in Great Britain, which limited the exportation of wheat and other grains. "Corn" was the word used to mean any grain or combination of grains used for food, be it wheat, oats, barley, etc. Of course what we think of as corn wasn't known about in the rest of the world until after the Americas began being discovered by Europeans, beginning in 1492, fifty-six years after the Corn Laws were passed.

Prior to refrigeration, one way beef was preserved was by salting it down. Bacteria can't live in salt. The salt used for that purpose was in large kernels, about the size of grain. Grain was called "corn." The size of the salt they used for rubbing down meat was the size of, and reminiscent of grain, such as wheat or barley. One rubbed the meat down with salt the size of "corn" and hence we have the ancient term, "corned beef." It simply meant that the beef had either been rubbed down with salt, or soaked in a salt-water solution, also called brine. I suppose it was easier to say something like, "I corned the beef," rather than, "I rubbed the beef down with kernels of salt the size of grain."

What we call corned beef today is normally the Point of Brisket, which is the larger and fatter end of the Brisket and the Plate. The meat is simply placed in a salt-water solution, a collection of spices, usually called "pickling spice," with a very small amount of sodium nitrite, and allowed to "cure" for several days or a week, depending on the thickness.

> **NOTE:** (Sodium nitrite and sodium nitrate are entirely different substances. Both have prevented infinitely more illness and death than any abuse of either ever could. The last time I bothered

to read a report on it by some fellow with a PhD in chemistry, I dismissed the article after seeing him use sodium nitrite and sodium nitrate interchangeably in the first two paragraphs. He didn't know the difference. Properly used, either one or both have been as important to the health and well being of mankind as anything we have.)

Being very chewy, tough if you will, Brisket needs a long slow cooking method, as does corned beef. While the most expensive portion of the Brisket, the Plate or Brisket Plate is very lean, it usually is dry as corned beef, and without much fat content, it isn't as flavorful. As the Brisket moves toward the hindquarter, the back portion of the Brisket becomes the Plate. The Plate portion of the Brisket is a thick, lean muscle, with very little marbling. It is sometimes sold as Brisket Plate, but it is also used for corned beef. It generally costs more per pound than the fatty point.

The upper portion of the Plate becomes progressively too fat to be used as Short Ribs or corned beef as you move toward the hindquarter. While the best and traditional Pastrami is made from the Point of the Brisket, the upper, fatter portion of the Plate is also commonly used for pastrami making. Simply smoking beef that has been corned makes pastrami.

## Shank

The Shank muscles surround the leg bone above the hoof and knee.

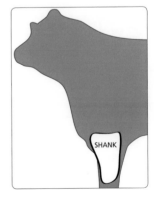

The Shank, front or rear, is a much-used set of muscles, with many tendons and sinews.

Shanks are typically cut across the leg bone, the meat left on, and used in soups or stews. The sinews break down into a gelatin at temperatures over about 215 degrees. The bone marrow adds to the flavor. Those Shanks that exceed the demand are boned out and the meat makes a very lean ground beef.

# The Hindquarter

Just as there are two front quarters per beef, there are two hindquarters. The hindquarter also has its primal cuts.

- **The Round** is essentially the entire rear leg. It extends from the shank to the pelvic bone.

- **The Sirloin Tip** muscle group runs from the rear knee up to the large knucklebone at the hip. The Sirloin Tip runs up the rear leg bone, and is separated from the round and the Head Loin.

- **The Full Loin** contains the Head Loin and the Short Loin, where T-Bone Steaks come from. The Filet originates in the Head Loin, and tapers out in the Short Loin. Above the pelvic bone, in the Head Loin, lies the Top Sirloin.

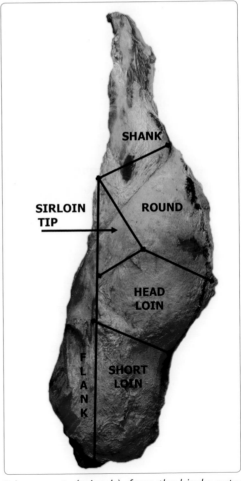

*Primary cuts (primals), from the hindquarter*

- **The Flank** contains steak that is coarsely grained, with long fibers that nicely absorb a flavorful marinade.

The photo below shows the general location of the primals as they were cut from the hanging hindquarter.

*Cuts from the hindquarter (L–R, top): Eye of Round, Full Bottom Round, Top Sirloin, Top Loin Strip (or New York Strip). (bottom center) Sirloin Tip*

In the photo above, my hand is holding the Eye of Round at the far left. Adjoining the Eye, to its right, is the full Bottom Round, followed by the Top Sirloin, and finally the New York Strip or Top Loin Strip. The Sirloin Tip, slightly out of place for demonstration purposes, connects the Bottom Round at its right edge, and the edge of the Top Round, only partly visible, under the Bottom Round. The photo excludes the Flank and the Shank. Each cut shown is a primal of the hindquarter, as they came from the counter of a chain store. They were unwrapped and rinsed for the photo, and laid out in the approximate location as they come from a hindquarter.

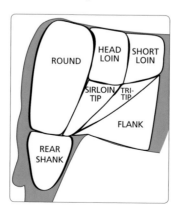

# Round

When a full quarter is hung, it's hung with the Shank at the top. On a hanging hindquarter, the Rear Shank is at the top.

As mentioned in the previous chapter, the Front Shank and Rear Shank are almost indistinguishable.

The Round begins at the Rear Shank. From here the Round divides into three main muscles: Top Round, Bottom Round and Eye of Round. The three muscles continue to the pelvic bone, where they end.

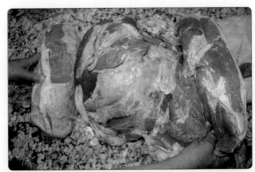

*L–R: Eye of Round, Top Round, Bottom Round*

## Top Round

The largest end of the Top Round sits at the pelvic bone. At this end, the Top Round is one large muscle—the inner thigh muscle.

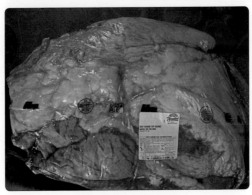

*Whole Top Round*

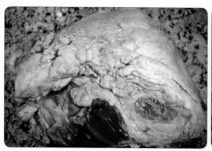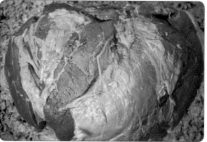

*(L) Unwrapped whole Top Round, exterior;*
*(R) Unwrapped whole Top Round, interior*

Down a few inches from this end, another muscle, less tender, joins the main muscle. It gets larger and tougher as you progress toward the knee. At this point, the main Top Round muscle is at its smallest, and is much less tender than where it began at the pelvic bone.

It's simple enough to slice a Top Round, but you will have some trimmings left over for making ground beef, stew or whatever you choose.

*Slicing a Top Round*

"London Broil" is actually a recipe, not a cut of meat. It implies broiling only to rare or medium rare, then slicing the thick steak into thin strips. Broiled and thinly sliced, this cut—the uppermost few inches of Top Round, where it began at the pelvic bone—is flavorful and somewhat easy to chew. Cooked through to medium or well done, it becomes a dry, chewy adventure in not-so-fine dining. Generally, because it's most tender at that end, only the top portion of the Top Round is labeled for London Broil. After the first few inches of the

Top Round, the steaks might better be used for some kind of Swiss steak, sliced very thinly for any number of uses, such as any braised beef recipe calling for very lean meat, stew meat, or even ground up for very lean ground beef.

## Bottom Round

*A Whole Bottom Round*

The Bottom Round and the adjacent Eye of Round, at the very rear of the hind leg, are much-used muscles.

In former days, the Rump Roast was a large, bone-in roast, which included a large portion of the pelvic bone and hip ball joint where the Top, Bottom, and Eye of Round muscles ended. Today, with mostly boneless primals arriving at retail markets, the only Rump Roast you're likely to find is in fact only the uppermost portion of the Bottom Round.

*Rump being cut from the Whole Bottom Round*

The remainder of the Bottom Round is often sliced and run through a meat-tenderizing machine, and called "Minute Steak", "Cubed Steak", "Chicken Fry Steak" or whatever might sell better in any given store. Like the lower portion of the Top Round, the Bottom Round is a much-used locomotion muscle. As such, it is tough and chewy unless it's cooked long and slow, or as described above under Top Round.

## Eye of Round

The Eye of Round, like the Top Round and Bottom Round muscles, runs from the pelvic bone down to the rear knee. It's the outermost muscle at the back of the leg and is adjacent on each side to the Top and Bottom Round muscles.

*Whole Eye of Round, packaged*

The Eye of Round is a much-used locomotion muscle, as it goes into use whenever the beef takes a step. The Eye of Round Roast has a lot of visual appeal because of its cylindrical shape, the absence of fat, and no bone. As a roast, it needs to be slow cooked with liquid or somehow tenderized. Oven-roasted to rare or medium rare, the Eye of Round is tough to chew.

Sometimes it is sliced into cute little round steaks and brazenly labeled "Breakfast Steak."

The slices, run through a commercial meat tenderizer several times to make them chewable, will be labeled "Chicken Fry Steaks", "Minute Steaks", etc., just as Bottom Round steaks might be tenderized and labeled.

## Tri-Tip

The Tri-Tip is a muscle, seemingly in suspension, somewhat at the juncture of the tip of the Sirloin Tip, the Top Round and the Top Sirloin.

This is another of the newer inventions of the advertising and marketing people. In days gone by, it was simply a part of the "tail" of the Sirloin Steak, or the Top Sirloin Steak. As such, as much of it as could be left on those steaks was simply left on them. The remaining "tail" was held aside for ground beef, cut into pieces as "stew meat," or cut into two-to-three ounce pieces and run through the tenderizing machine for "Cube Steak," "Minute Steak," "Chicken Fry Steak," or whatever the name might be more popular at any given market.

Removed whole, the Tri-Tip muscle generally weighs 1.5 to 2.5 pounds if it's taken from average-sized beef cattle. I've seen some very large ones lately, at acceptable special prices, in the range of 3 to 4.5 pounds. The relatively enormous ones that I've seen have much more exterior fat than the smaller ones. They've been well marbled, and those I've London Broiled (covered with Lawry's Garlic Salt, grilled over medium heat for half hour on each side, allowed to rest five to ten minutes and thinly sliced across the grain) have been a big hit.

Tri-Tips have large muscle fibers that aren't tightly connected. As such, this cut absorbs marinades and seasonings more readily and more freely than say the Top Sirloin, Sirloin Tip and Top Round, which contain tightly compacted muscle fibers. While the Tri-Tip can generally be described as somewhat "tender," without seasonings it has a very mild flavor.

# Sirloin Tip

The Sirloin Tip runs along the upper leg bone, in a front of the Top and Bottom Round. It is removed by sliding a knife down the full length of the leg bone running from the rear knee joint down to where the ball joint at the end of the leg bone meets the hipbone socket.

This muscle group, being the front portion of the rear leg, and well worked in the animal's walking and running, is known as a locomotion muscle. For that reason, there is very little internal fat and usually no visible marbling.

*Whole Sirloin Tip in package*

## Top Sirloin

You can often buy a whole Top Sirloin right out of the self-serve counter.

*The large end of the Top Sirloin*

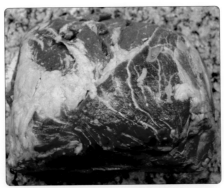

*Whole Top Sirloin from the top*

*Small end of Top Sirloin*

The Top Sirloin shown in the photos wasn't aged at all, as I normally would age a full Top Sirloin. (More about aging later, but I take it out of the plastic wrap, rinse with cold tap water, put it on a sheet of freezer wrap, plastic side up, on the shelf of a refrigerator for at least ten days, preferably twenty to thirty days.)

You can age your beef or not, of course, as you like. If you simply take the Whole Top Sirloin out of the package, rinse it and let it sit at least over night in the fridge, you can start using it immediately. You can just cut off what you need and put the remainder back in the refrigerator. If you do that, just pat a sheet of plastic food wrap over the end you've cut from to keep it from drying out. Or, as you like, you can cut it all into steaks, tightly double wrap each of them, tightly zip lock or vacuum seal them and freeze them for later use.

*Cutting into a Top Sirloin*

*First cut*

*Second cut*

*Top Sirloin all cut into steaks*

*The smallest end of the Sirloin*

Note that the steaks from the large end of the Head Loin, nearest the Rump and Round, contain heavy sinews near the center. This knot of sinew is easily simply cut out with no harm done.

*Sinew in Top Sirloin*

*Knot of sinew removed*

The smallest Top Sirloin Steak is the steak that would be followed immediately by the large end of the Beef Loin Strip, or New York Strip.

*The smallest Top Sirloin Steak*

*New York Strip as it connects to the Top Sirloin*

The large end may be more suitable for London Broil. Taken from USDA Prime or Choice beef, and very often from USDA Select beef, the Top Sirloin is generally tender enough to broil or grill.

Toward the smaller end of the Top Sirloin, the individual steaks would almost always be expected to be tender enough for grilling or broiling as an individual, traditional "steak."

There is no 100% guarantee that because a beef has been graded any given grade that it will be relatively tough or relatively tender—or that it won't be. For instance, I grilled the largest the USDA Select Top Sirloin Steaks shown here to medium-rare. To my great surprise they were as tender as any steak I've ever had.

On the other hand, probably the most picture-perfect USDA Choice Blade Cut Chuck Roast I've ever seen was just plain tough. It was beautifully marbled, perfectly filled out muscles, perfectly shaped, and of ideal fat content. While cutting a number of chucks into roast while working for Safeway, I had set it aside for myself. Oven-roasted to perfection, it was so tough that it was inedible. While these are both very unlikely and unusual occurrences, it does sometimes happen.

In days gone by, the Head Loin was often simply sliced whole into Full Sirloin Steaks. (If you're curious about what that looked like, it was almost exactly the appearance of a Sirloin Lamb Chop, or a Loin End Pork Chop. You can see the Tenderloin in either, running on the lower side of the pelvic bone. Of course a full beef Sirloin Steak would be more the area of a very large chuck roast.)

## The Filet

The Filet runs from the beginning of the Head Loin, at the joint of the hip bone and pelvic bone, along the underside of the pelvic bone, and tapers down as it continues along the Head Loin, into the Short Loin. It continues to taper and becomes smaller until it ends a few inches from the small end of the Short Loin.

Generally the Filet is removed before slicing, but was sometimes left in, which made an enormous and rather confused steak. The full Sirloin Steak of yesteryear included the Top Sirloin—which is not generally considered to be the most tender steak—a cross-section of the pelvic bone, and the largest cross section of the Filet Steak, the most tender of any steak on the beef.

*This package contains the Filet Butt portions of two whole filets.*

*Unwrapped Filet Butt*

*The underside of the Filet Butt*

The "Butt End Filet" is that largest portion of the Filet, from its beginning at the hipbone to its ending at the end of the pelvic bone. Above the pelvic bone is the Top Sirloin.

Sometimes cooked whole, the Butt End Filet is that cut used for "Chateaubriand", "Beef Wellington" and a variety of recipes where it is enclosed in a pastry crust and meant to serve several people.

The photo below shows the relationship of the Top Sirloin and the Butt end of the Filet. The pelvic bone is all that separated the two.

*The Filet sitting above the Top Sirloin*

The Filet, or Filet Mignon Steak, is the least used muscle and therefore most tender steak on the beef. The word "mignon" is a French word meaning small. The word "filet" implies, "without bone." The Filet contains little marbling, therefore not as much flavor as some other cuts from the same beef. Because the Filet is extremely tender, it is highly favored.

On a 275-pound side of beef, the entire Filet will ordinarily weigh no more than six or seven pounds, making its supply less than the demand there is for it.

The meat fibers in the Filet are less tightly packed. For that reason, in part, the Filet will cook more rapidly than any other steak. You may have noticed that if you've had Porterhouse or T-Bone Steaks; the Filet portion is "well done" while the New York portion of the steak is "medium rare."

When the boneless whole or butt portion of a Filet arrives at the retail market, it has no protective bone or fat encompassing it. For that reason, it won't age well at all, and aging it really isn't necessary. You could simply unwrap and rinse, let it rest a day or two under refrigeration, and cook it whole or slice it into steaks as you like.

### To Make the Most of a Whole Sirloin Tip

1.  Open the package over the sink and give it a good rinse.

2.   Remove as much of the outer sinew as possible.

*Remove the sinew*

3.   Cut the Sirloin Tip right down the center, from the top.

Note that one side is solid, called the "silver side," or "solid side," because of the silvery color of the sinewy connective tissue covering it, and because it is one solid piece of muscle.

*In the photo above, the Silver Side is on the left.*

*Slicing the solid side*

*Thick-cut steak on the left;*
*thin-cut steaks on the right*

The silver side is usually cut into steaks, as seen in the photos, either thickly or very thinly. Thinly cut, the steaks from either the solid side or soft side of the Sirloin Tip can be used for any number of recipes calling for very thin, fatless slices of beef, such as Carne Asada, Scaloppini, or any recipe you might ordinarily use for preparing a Top Round Steak.

The other half of the Sirloin Tip is called the "soft side."

*The soft side is where most of the sinew sits*

*Removing more sinew from the soft side*

*Getting off the last bit of sinew*

After removing all the thicker sinews possible, the soft side of the Sirloin Tip can be tied into a Sirloin Tip Roast.

*Tying the soft side into a roast*

As it is very poorly marbled and a much-used muscle, the Sirloin Tip Roast might be better pot roasted or braised. It would also make an acceptable oven roast or rotisserie roast, were it well seasoned before tying, wrapped first in parchment paper, and that package wrapped in aluminum foil.

## Full Loin

The Full Loin contains the Head Loin and the Short Loin.

The Head Loin, removed from just in front of the Rump (or Round), is then separated from the Short Loin.

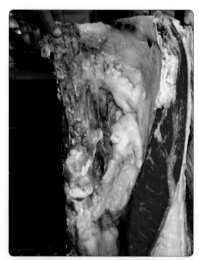

*A Full Loin that has been separated from the Round.*

*A hanging hindquarter with the Flank being pulled away from the Full Loin.*

The photo above shows the inside of a hanging hindquarter with the Flank pulled back. The portion visible is the Full Loin. The white ball of fat at the lower right contains the Kidney. The individual vertebrae along the backbone are facing outward. The approximate upper 40% of the whole loin is the Head Loin, and below that, beginning at the very end of the pelvic bone, lays the Short Loin.

## Head Loin

The Head Loin contains most of the pelvic bone. Along the underside of the pelvic bone is located the large major portion of the Filet, or the "butt" of the Filet. Above the pelvic bone lies the Top Sirloin.

## Short Loin

The remainder of the Full Loin is the Short Loin. The Short Loin begins at the end of the pelvic bone, where the Top Sirloin ends. It ends at the small end of the Rib. The Short Loin contains the remaining tapering Filet on the underside of the backbone, and below the short, broad flat bones that extend down from the spine. The Filet tapers down to nothing a few inches from the end of the Short Loin.

Above the flat bones extending down from the spine, and the spine bone itself, lays the entire New York Strip, or Loin Strip. Cut whole, with the bone in, the large end of the Short Loin becomes Porterhouse Steaks. As the Filet tapers down, those steaks that have some portion of the Filet are called T-Bone Steaks. The spine bone and the flat broad bones that extend down from the spine form the T in the T-Bone Steak.

*Typical T-bone Steak*

A typical T-bone Steak as shown above contains a portion of the spinal vertebrae. The bone completing the T separates the New York (Loin) from the Filet.

*The knife points to the Filet portion of the T-bone.*

The steaks made from the end of the Short Loin, where the filet has tapered down to nothing, with the bone left in, are often called "Club Steaks" or "Bone-in New York Steaks." In some markets, Bone-in New York Steak will sell for a few cents more than if it's called Club Steak. In other markets, Club Steak, will sell for more than a Bone-in New York Steak. Without the bone, the steak is called a New York Steak, New York Strip Steak, or "Boneless Loin Steak." It really isn't a New York Steak or New York Strip if there's a bone involved, but at least we know where it came from.

*An ungraded Bone-in New York Strip Steak*

The "New York Strip Steaks Bone-in," pictured above are from ungraded beef. Were they graded, the label would say USDA Choice, USDA Select, or whatever it might be. As this beef would never have been graded even USDA Select, it wasn't graded at all. The best that can be said about it is that it was "USDA Inspected." As you can see, there's virtually no marbling, the meat is light in color and feels 'soft' in the package. With true New York Steaks, the bones are easily removed.

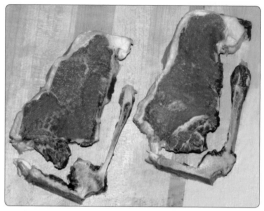

*Ungraded New York Strip steaks with the bones removed*

As these steaks were $3.99 per lb., the bones, at 4 oz., cost $1.00.

For instance, the Blade Chuck Roast below was well shaped, well marbled, had good color, and was thick. It was on sale for a total price of $4.86 at $1.57 per pound.

*Pictured above are three steaks that I cut from a large Blade Chuck Roast. Compare to the packaged Spencer Steak at the top.*

If you compare the boneless USDA Select Eye of Chuck Steaks below for color, you can see the deep rich red, well-marbled meat, compared to the pale color of the "Bone-in New York Steaks."

*USDA Select Eye of Chuck Steaks*

I've often wondered about the popularity of a Porterhouse or T-Bone Steak. The Porterhouse, which is the first two or three steaks from the Short Loin, is of course large in surface area.

Those first steaks, immediately nearest the Head Loin, are where both the New York and Filet steaks are at the largest. My guess is that in days gone by people were well pleased with a very large beefsteak. The problem is that the Filet portion of the Porterhouse or the T-Bone cooks much more rapidly than the New York portion of the steak.

If I want my steak medium rare, the New York, above the bone, may be medium rare, but the Filet is going to be well done. As I personally don't think the Filet has much flavor to begin with, the well-done Filet, on the other side of my medium rare New York side of the T-bone, is not going to please me much. Likewise, those who prefer the Filet portion aren't generally that fond of the larger New York on the other side of the bone. If the Filet is cooked to their satisfaction, the New York portion of the steak, above the bone, simply can't be.

We see a Top Round Steak labeled "London Broil" in the counter for say, $2.99 per lb., and next to that we see a thick Top Sirloin Steak on sale for $2.19 per lb. Both are from the same USDA grade of beef. The London Broil is most often a Top Round steak, from the large end of the top round.

Before pretty much everything went boneless, that portion of the Top Round Steak labeled "London Broil" was part of the bone-in Rump Roast. A Top Sirloin Steak, minus the small but annoyingly un-chewable connective tissue in the center of the large end, will be just as, if not more, flavorful—and generally much more tender than the top round, which is boldly labeled "London Broil."

Variously called "New York Steak", "Boneless New York Steak", "Bone-in New York Steak", "Loin Steak", "Bone-in Loin Steak", "Club Steak", "Bone-in Loin Steak" and/or such other as may be invented all refer to the same muscle—the top portion of the Short Loin. The Short Loin is that part of the hindquarter that runs from where the pelvic bone ends, to the twelfth rib up from the neck. In that location, this muscle isn't much used, and is one of the tenderest cuts on the beef.

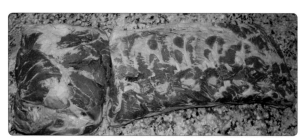

*Relationship of Top Sirloin and New York Strip*

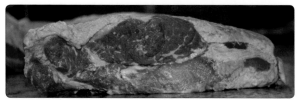

*The large end of the New York Strip where it was severed from the Head Loin. Note the white traces of sinew, which were the very ends of the pelvic bone.*

As the Short Loin moves toward the front, toward the rib, the New York Strip becomes slightly smaller, and the filet tapers to nothing a few inches before reaching the twelfth rib back from the neck, which is the beginning of the Rib.

Where the Filet, sometimes called Tenderloin, runs out, it is cut into steaks with the bone left in, and may be called Club Steak, Bone-in New York Steak, Bone-in Shell Steak, Shell Steak, Bone-in Loin Steak, or by whatever other name might sell best in that particular market.

Regardless of the name on the package, if the steak came from the Short Loin, it's either the Filet (Tenderloin), or it's the top of the loin, most commonly called a New York Steak or a New York Strip. "Bone-in New York Steak," or "Boneless New York Steak," ("boneless" being redundant), this cut is normally lightly marbled with little interior fat. It's generally considered as tender as any steak on the beef, with the exception of the Filet. It's normally the second most expensive steak, following only the Filet.

The New York Steak is popular because it is boneless, tender, and generally flavorful. The marbling in the New York is adequate, though not as well marbled as the Rib from the same beef. From a USDA Choice hindquarter, the New York Steak is ideal for broiling or grilling. Like any other meat, it can be made tough and dry by over-cooking, but can generally be broiled or grilled to a just "well done" state without being overly tough and dry.

## Flank

The Flank, containing one Flank Steak and "Flap Meat," is removed from the hindquarter with one long slice.

There are two Flank Steaks per each whole beef—one on each flank. The Flank Steak is coarsely grained, with long fibers. It has a distinctive though mild flavor and can be marinated and grilled, or cooked slowly. If it is to be marinated and broiled or grilled, it shouldn't be cooked to more than medium rare. It should be thinly sliced across the grain, as you would a London Broil.

Cut thickly or with the grain rather than across it, it's going to be a jaw exercise. Of course there are any number of recipes that use a Flank Steak that include braising or long slow cooking to well done, which would tenderize it nicely.

"Flap Meat" is a lean section of meat within the flank. The photo below exhibits the red strip of meat which is where the whole Flank was removed. The continuation of that red strip is where "Flap Meat" comes from.

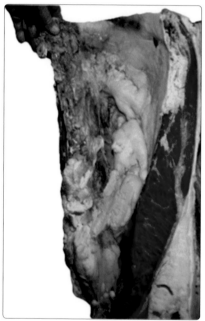

*The red streak of meat is where the Flank was removed.*

# Why Buy a Primal?

There are some national and regional stores that offer whole primals in the self-service counters. Costco, for instance, carries USDA Choice Beef, and regularly has whole New York Strips, boneless Rib Eyes, Sirloin Tips and Filets, among others, in vacuum-sealed plastic wrap, just as they were received from the meat processing plant.

I almost never buy steaks, roasts, or anything else for that matter, that have already been cut. There are several reasons:

1. It hasn't been exposed to the open air while in transit.

2. It hasn't been handled since it was removed from the carcass and vacuum-sealed in the plastic wrap. It's as sanitary and as bacteria free as it can possibly be. This factor alone is important enough to me to buy that way, even if there were no other reasons.

3. Since it hasn't been cut into or sliced, the natural juiciness isn't absorbed into the pad at the bottom of individual meat tray.

4. The price is usually dramatically cheaper.

5. I can age it myself.

6. I can use the various sections of a Boneless Chuck or a whole Sirloin Tip for any variety of steaks, roasts, ground beef, etc., as I choose.

7. I can cut the roasts the size I want.

8. I can cut the steaks as thick or thin as I like, and immediately freeze them so they don't lose their juiciness.

9.   I can age those cuts that are improved with aging. Almost any cut of beef is improved with aging.

## When Buying a Primal

When beef is properly cooled after slaughter, good beef is much harder than poor beef.

Since the primals available to the public and those received by the markets were vacuum-sealed before the beef had fully cooled, the meat is still soft. When you unwrap it and put it in your refrigerator, you'll notice that the meat is much more solid to the touch a day later. The fat within the meat has hardened. As the primals have been stripped of most of the exterior fat, when selecting a primal such as a Boneless Rib Eye or New York Strip, if you gently squeeze the lower end, just below the eye, you can feel roughly how much fat you can't see. The fat will be a hard mass. I check the fat content in that location because I want to know how much excess fat I'm going to get. If it has an excessively large mass of fat that will have to be removed, I move on to the next. You'll often be able to feel a dramatic difference in that fat mass between the usually smaller, whole Boneless Rib Eye that came from a heifer, and a usually larger Boneless Rib Eye from a steer.

As the beef wasn't properly cooled before packaging, the marbling content is very hard to determine. The marbling won't be fully apparent until the meat is removed from the vacuum seal and allowed to cool. You can get a fair idea from the marbling you can see, but you should know that there will be more than what you can see through the vacuum sealed package.

After I check for excess fat within the package and determine how well the meat might be marbled, I look for the fullness of the muscle. If it's well rounded, I know the beef was well fed and mature. If I'm buying USDA Choice beef, the differences between three or four different "Boneless Rib Eyes" might be quite large. Sometimes there will be up to five pounds in weight difference between them, and in every case

I buy the largest one in the counter. First, I have complete trust in USDA graders, and second, the largest, most well developed muscle is virtually always from a large steer, meaning the meat is going to be very adequately marbled and will have minimal excess fat outside the main "eye."

In buying a USDA Select graded primal, I follow the same criteria. If the beef isn't graded at all, there won't be much marbling and I only look for color, muscle fullness, and overall size.

# Consider the Meat Ads

With most grocery shopping done on weekends, markets generally advertise their specials on Thursdays, hoping to lure shoppers to their stores with bargain priced items. Knowing that most shoppers will buy most or all their groceries in the same store they buy their meat, generally the meat specials are to be found on the first page of any advertising page.

The three meaningful things you need to know are:

- **USDA Inspected?**

  Often that's the only description on the quality of a cut of meat. Of course the USDA inspected it. It's highly illegal to sell any beef that wasn't inspected by the USDA. If it's in a commercial meat counter, you can be certain the USDA inspected it.

- **What is the USDA Grade?**

  Any other descriptive words are meaningless. If the beef is USDA Choice or USDA Select, or USDA Prime, it will carry that seal. If the beef wasn't graded by a USDA grader, the reason is that it either would not have graded USDA Select or higher and so wasn't graded at all.

  Prestigious sounding store brands or flowery adjectives won't change the quality of what it is. Don't be lulled into thinking that the beef in this meat counter was "Selected," "Reserved," or any other marketing adjectives that were created to make you believe something that isn't true.

- **Which primal did it come from?**

"Milanesa," "Asada," "London Broil," etc., are all recipes. If you know from where on the beef the cut came, you can have a very good idea of how it might best be prepared and can choose your own recipe. Fat and bone aside, I personally think a Chuck Roast makes a better London Broil than any Top Round Steak.

## What is Steak?

Steak is defined as "a slice of meat cut for cooking or broiling." The word comes from the Old Norse word *steik*, meaning a slice of meat roasted on a spit. Today we find advertising for all kinds of beef products calling almost any cut of meat "steak." Advertising tells us that their hamburgers aren't simply ground beef; they're "ground steakburgers." Tacos contain "steak," and now we find that the beef in a can of soup is actually "steak." It seems that using the word "steak" adds value, whether it's ground beef in a taco or hamburger, or in a can with beans. Since the word "steak" simply means a slice of meat, it's fair enough to call a slice of bacon or a slice of shank meat "steak." I doubt if anyone could tell the difference between a slice of beef from the neck, shank, rib, loin, or any other slice of beef with more or less the same fat content once it's gone through a grinder. Chopped into small pieces and cooked in a soup, taco or burger, I couldn't tell you from where it came. Nor would I care.

When we generally think of steak, we think of one that can be successfully grilled or broiled without going to extremes: Filet, New York, Porterhouse, T-Bone, Rib Eye, Rib, and Top Sirloin. Abuse of the word for marketing purposes, giving the illusion that we're getting something special because it's called "steak" causes the word to lose any meaning the word might have. Maybe we should just change the name of "beef" to "steak."

# Today's Ads

- **Buy One, Get One Free**

Promoting "select" chicken parts, that sounds like a great deal! It fades though when you see the "regular price" has been nearly doubled for this particular "sale."

- **Angus Choice T-bone or Boneless New York Steaks**

This one has the USDA Choice logo following the price of $8.99 per pound, so you know it is that grade. I doubt anyone can tell the difference in the flavor between a USDA Choice Angus steak, and the same steak from a USDA Choice Hereford.

- **Black Angus**

Long considered by many to be the best of the beef breeds, there is a marketing effort underway to elevate the value of Angus. It may be true that a herd of Black Angus will produce overall a superior beef than some other breeds under the same conditions. The problem, if anyone could tell the difference in any given cut of beef, is that the term 'Angus,' or 'Black Angus,' has been sorely abused. Most Angus producers today consider any cattle that are 51% black haired to be Angus. If the illusion can be created to make us think we're actually getting purebred Angus, we'll be willing to pay more. It's doubtful that any Angus beef carried by a chain grocery store contains high percentages of Angus DNA. If what I see is USDA Choice, and that's the grade I want in the cut I'm buying, I really don't care what color its hair was.

- **Fresh Beef T-bone or New York Steaks**

This was in the window adjoining the Angus T-bone ad, at $6.99 per pound, $2.00 per pound less than the USDA Choice Angus Steak. There is no grade stated on the $6.99 ad, meaning it is probably ungraded. The same steaks are offered at another store, in the same week, from USDA Select graded beef, for $3.99 per pound. Those offered at $6.99 certainly aren't USDA Choice or Select, or the ad would say it was. Alongside the higher priced Angus, it looks like a remarkable deal; and it further supports the price of $8.99 for the USDA Choice Angus Steaks. The price of $8.99 per pound for USDA Choice T-Bone and New York Steaks is a fair price. However, why would you pay $6.99 for apparently ungraded steaks when you could buy the same steaks from USDA Select beef for $3.99 down the street?

I bought a whole, well trimmed, USDA Choice New York Strip, weighing fifteen pounds, for $6.59 per pound, and a whole, well trimmed, USDA Choice Rib for $5.59, at Costco, on the same day as this came out. At $3.40 per pound less, I'll take the fifteen-pound New York Strip and have far superior steaks with a total savings of $51.00!

- **Beef Rib Eye Steaks, on sale for $3.99/lb.**

There is no grade shown. In the finer print below, it says, "bone-in." Of course there can't be "bone-in" Rib Eye Steaks. If they're bone-in, they're Rib Steaks. The Eye of Rib is the center muscle of the Rib. No bone is or ever was present in the Rib Eye.

Just below that, the same chain store ad is introducing a new store line of special very prestigious-sounding beef. Producers who, by the sound of the very prestigious name of their company, really know their stuff, are bringing it to us from some mid-western state. They're offering "Angus Choice Beef Rib Eye Steaks," (bone-in) for $5.99 per pound, $2.00 per pound more than the other un-graded "Beef Rib Eye Steaks," with the bone-in. It says "'Angus Choice." It doesn't say USDA Choice. If the ad did say USDA Choice, it would mean something you could rely on. They could call USDA Canner-graded beef "Choice." In this case, we have no way of knowing what the grade of any of this beef might have been. The producers of this meat and the retailer didn't want any pesky certified USDA grader putting a USDA grade on it.

- **(Store Brand) New York Steaks, on sale at $3.47/lb.**

This from another chain grocery store; in the fine print beneath it says, "bone-in." "New York Steak" has always implied that the steak was boneless. Since these steaks are not labeled USDA Choice, USDA Select, etc., they're from ungraded beef. Giving them some kind of apparently prestigious brand name makes us think they're somehow more special than any other ungraded beef, and therefore more valuable.

- **Boneless Beef Tri-Tip**

This is offered, again un-graded with this chain store's brand name only, at $4.99—but it's "boneless." That's implied, isn't it? There isn't a bone anywhere near the vicinity of a Tri-Tip. A competitor had Tri-Tips on sale the week before for $1.99. Very large for Tri-Tips, they weighed up to 4.5 pounds. They were un-trimmed, had some excess fat, but they were well marbled, no doubt from very large steers. I bought a dozen—and they're excellent! Tri-Tips from average-sized beef cattle would ordinarily not weigh more than about 2.5 pounds. With a very mild flavor, Tri-Tips are not tightly compacted muscles, as are the muscles of the Round: Top, Bottom and Eye, or the Sirloin Tip. Loosely grained, the Tri-Tip much more readily absorbs seasonings than tightly grained cuts.

- **Boneless Beef Cross Rib Steaks available at $2.99/lb.**

Even from highly graded beef, the Cross Rib, or Shoulder Clod from the much-used shoulder is not considered a "tender" location of the beef. It's always boneless, so pointing that out isn't necessary; it just makes it sound like a better deal. Not well marbled, and containing some heavy sinews, this cut is not generally thought of for ordinary broiling or grilling. It does have an excellent flavor. It would be much more on par with a Top Round rather than a Rib Steak as to tenderness. A competing store offers "Boneless Beef Shoulder Clod Steak," for $1.79 per pound. That store however has no brand name for its beef. This is also apparently un-graded beef; no different than the same cut that is offered for $2.99 but in a disguise of meaningless adjectives.

• **Boneless Beef Round Steaks on sale at $3.49/lb.**

It doesn't say whether it's Top Round, Bottom Round, or Eye of Round. Again, no grade, but only the stores brand name. Just below that, Boneless Beef Top Round London Broil can be purchased for the same price.

"Boneless" is implied if it's Top Round, "London Broil" is a recipe. What this ad offers, with the fluffy and prestigious adjectives removed, is ungraded Round Steaks, probably all Top Rounds. Since the Top Round portion nearest the pelvic bone is most commonly called London Broil, they would be more tender than from the lower portion of the leg, or Round, muscle. As such, at the same price, they're the better buy of the two. The main difference is in size. People not wanting the always thicker cut London Broil portion of the Top Round, or not wanting to buy a two- or three-pound Top Round Steak, will buy a thinner and smaller Top Round Steak from the lower portion of the leg, which is typically a comparatively tough steak.

One might London broil a Top Round Steak from the uppermost portion of the Top Round, slice it thinly, and expect it to be reasonably tender. From the lower end of the same full Top Round, it wouldn't be nearly as tender.

- **Boneless Beef Top Sirloin or Ground Beef Sirloin, 90% lean**

Offered at $2.99 per pound, no grade, alongside the same USDA Choice Angus Top Sirloin for $3.99 per pound. Again, each price pulls up the apparent value of the other. In fact both prices are pretty usual, but the illusion created in placing the ads as they are is that both appear to be great values.

If you want 90% lean ground beef, you might want to grind a Top, Bottom, or Eye of Round, usually on sale for $1.00 less per pound. Is there any difference after it's ground? None that I can tell.

You might want 85% lean, 90% lean, or even higher in your ground beef. It's the fat content of meat that gives it flavor. I think most chefs and cooks agree that about 75% lean is ideal for that "juicy" and flavorful Hamburger.

While I'm on that page of advertisements, let me digress a moment to point out something about pork chops that might be of use to you.

Advertised here are "Boneless Pork Loin Center Cut Chops," offered at only $3.99 per pound. By comparison, very often at this store you can buy a whole boneless, very well trimmed pork loin weighing six to eight pounds, for $1.99 per pound.

There's virtually no waste. It's nothing at all to unwrap it over the sink, rinse it off, put it in the fridge unwrapped for a few hours or overnight, just long enough for it to harden a little, and slice it into twenty, thirty or forty pork chops, depending on how thickly you might like to slice them. You can trim each chop individually as much or little as you like.

You'll need to tightly double wrap as many as you want per package, in plastic wrap. Those you aren't going to use in the next day or two, should be enclosed in a zip lock bag or vacuum sealer or some such, and frozen. They say you shouldn't keep pork frozen for more than about three months. We have them every once in awhile that got lost in the freezer a year or two earlier. After they've thawed, I can only tell they've been frozen. After they're seasoned, breaded and fried or baked, we can't tell them from any that had never been frozen.

I'd much rather pay $16.00 for eight pounds of boneless pork chops than $32.00 for those cut by someone else a day or two earlier. After they're cut, the juices start to drain, meaning tougher, drier, more flavor-free pork chops. You'll have much better pork chops if you cut them and use them and/or freeze them for later.

# Cooking

There are basically only a few ways we cook meat:

- broil

- fry

- boil

- oven roast (dry or with liquid)

- pot roast with liquid

Grilling is essentially broiling, and pot-roasting with liquid is essentially boiling. We can smoke it and dry roast it slowly. We can fry it, with or without first "breading it" as in "chicken fried," or we can roast it fast or slow, to rare inside or well done, according to our taste.

COOKING TIP: To bring back the full flavor of any roasted, broiled or fried beef (or almost any other meat), put it in a steaming basket and steam it for a few minutes. If you don't already reheat leftover meat this way, you'll be amazed!

## Pot Roast

Pot Roast is not a cut of meat, but a recipe. We cook it in a pot with liquid. Any roast that is known to be tough or stringy should be cooked that way. When meat is cooked to about 215 F., internal temperature, the sinews, tough and un-chewable in meat that is to be grilled, broiled, or served less well cooked become gelatinized—easily chewed and a good source of calcium.

Most suitable cuts for pot roasting:

- Bottom Round Roast

- Larger end of the Chuck, where the 7-bone is small and barely recognizable as a "7" or it isn't there at all, meaning it's actually the neck.

- Eye of Round Roast

- Boneless Rump Roast (today that implies only the upper end of the Bottom Round)

## Oven Roast

Depending on the quality or grade of beef, we generally think of a Standing Rib, Blade Cut Chuck Roast, Top Sirloin or Cross Rib as suitable for oven roasting, that is, without moisture.

As the shoulder blade bone progresses, it fans out from it's socket. As it does, it appears as a number 7 when cut, and progresses to where it fans out into a "blade."

*(L) The 7-Bone Roast takes its name from the shape of the bone, not from the number of bones in the roast. (R) Blade Chuck Roast—note the white cartilage .*

As it nears the Rib, it is flat, and progress to white cartilage, which you often see in a "Blade Cut Chuck Roast" or "Chuck Steak." On a whole beef rib, before the "cap" is removed, the last two or three inches of that cartilage is present.

*Cap meat being removed from an Eye of Chuck.*

As referred to above, we very rarely see a whole beef rib anymore, and the "cap" has been taken off. Along with it, most of the outer fat and the white cartilage of the end of the blade bone has been removed.

The point is that when you see that the blade bone is flat and turning to cartilage in a Chuck Roast, you know it came from very near the Rib.

As the Rib is generally considered very tender and the most flavorful cut of beef, the Chuck at the point it is separated from the Rib is the best of the Chuck Roasts for marbling, tenderness and flavor. It may contain more fat, but overall, I personally think it's the tastiest and most tender oven roast, second only to a Rib Roast. Boneless or bone in, you might want to consider it for a London Broil. The meat on the outside of the blade tends to be "tough," and I just remove the blade bone and outer meat before cooking. I'll make ground beef out of that later, or cut it up into small pieces for some other use.

If you want it entirely boneless, it's easy enough to just slide your knife along the remaining bone. You can cut the little bit of remaining meat from the removed bones and use it however you like, or leave that bit of meat on the remaining bones and make soup, beef stock, etc.

# "Chicken Fry" Tip

With so much of our cooking turned over to the "junk food" and pre-packaged meals industries, I shouldn't be so surprised to find that most people today who haven't cooked much but who are now starting to cook more have the steps involved in "chicken fried" backward. If you intend to "chicken fry" any meat—be it fish, chicken, pork chops or a cubed/tenderized beef steak, you need to first flour the meat. Without the flour, the egg wash (egg beaten with water or milk) won't adhere to meat.

After flouring the meat, the meat is then dipped in egg wash, then dredged in bread or cracker crumbs. From there it should be refrigerated for at least half an hour, or even a day or two, before frying. I always put my seasonings on before I flour the meat. I often bread two or three chickens, fry only what we'll have for dinner and tomorrow's lunch, then tightly wrap the remainder and put it in the freezer. The individual pieces won't stick together even though they're not separated within the package. I just let it thaw, carefully separate the pieces, and fry it just as I would fry anything. It's impossible to tell the difference between freshly breaded and fried chicken, and the fried chicken that was breaded two months ago.

## Cooking Chuck

What else can you can easily do?

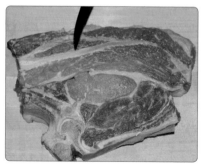

*This USDA Select Blade Cut Chuck Roast was actually labeled "7-Bone Chuck Roast."*

A 7-Bone Chuck Roast normally sells for more than a Blade Cut Chuck Roast, but as 7-Bone Roasts were on sale, there was no price difference. Notice the white cartilage, called the "blade," which is located toward the point that separates the Chuck from the Rib. At this end of the shoulder blade bone, there are a few inches of this cartilage, which shows you how near to the Rib the Blade Cut Chuck Roast was located. Of course, being adjacent to the Rib, this will always be the tenderest and best marbled of the Chuck Roasts.

If you want to have several uses from this cut, just remove the bones and separate the roast at the seams, sinews, and you'll have isolated several different muscles.

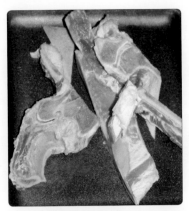

*Chuck Roast bones*

*Splitting an Eye of Chuck into two steaks.*
*The upper portion will make a very flavorful*
*and acceptable steak just as shown.*

If you prefer, you can slide your knife blade around it quite easily and then split it into two or more thinner steaks.

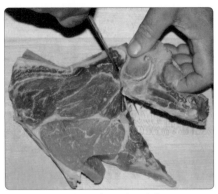

*Removing the Chuck bone*

The meat between the Eye and the Blade bone won't be nearly as tender. You may prefer to make stew or ground beef with that, or any number of other recipes that might not call for very tender beef.

*A true 7-Bone Roast*

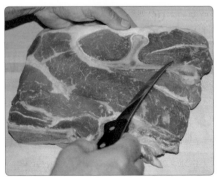

*Another 7-Bone Roast (the "7" is reversed on this side of the roast)*

You might prefer to remove only the 7 bone.

*Removing the Flat Iron Steak from the roast*

*Continuing the Flat Iron cut*

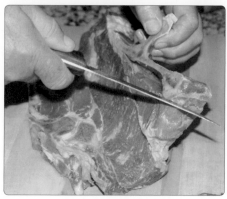

*Removing the 7 bone*

Or you can remove all of the bones.

*Removing the rest of the bones*

*Taking out the final bone*

*A 7-Bone Roast with bones removed and isolated separate muscles*

You might then wish to just cook the whole thing boneless as it is, or you might want to divide it up into its various distinctly different muscles.

When buying beef, if you know what primal the cut came from, you can decide if it's suitable for how you intend to prepare it.

Consider, if you will, that a live beef on the hoof is moving around a 1,000-pound body, and that it takes some pretty strong muscles to do that. The front and rear legs and shoulders are "locomotion muscles," meaning they move the animal with every step it takes. The meat from the legs and shoulders will have very little fat or marbling. Meat without fat or marbling will have less flavor, tend to dry out quickly when cooked, and generally be considered "tough." The hind legs are called Rounds in their primal form.

As you move up the beef and toward the center of the animal, the muscles are less used. In the center of the beef, the Loin and Rib are most tender; most marbled, and thus better flavored. Consumer demand is the only determining factor in the price per pound of any given cut of meat.

Moving toward the tail, the Loin muscle becomes larger, more used, and we call the continuing muscle the Top Sirloin where the pelvic bone ends. As the Loin muscle has become larger and tougher, the marbling has all but disappeared in the Top Sirloin Steak.

Moving from the center of the beef, (the dividing point between what we call the Short Loin, at the beginning of the Hindquarter, and the Rib) at the beginning of the Front Quarter, toward the head, the muscles become more used again. The large end of the Rib, where the shoulder blade ends with a strip of cartilage, becomes the Blade Chuck Roast. Continuing, the shoulder blade has become larger, shaped like a 7, before it disappears altogether from the Chuck. The Chuck Roast which has only a portion of the spinal column at one edge, is actually more Neck than Chuck. The neck holds up the beef's head 24/7. The neck meat is poorly marbled and as "tough" and "stringy" as any on the beef.

The "Shoulder Clod," "X-Rib," "Round Bone Roast," or by whatever names the front shoulder might be called, immediately adjoining the front leg, or shank, is a much used muscle. Absent much marbling, the front shoulder can make a fine oven roast if it's properly prepared.

## Things to Consider

We're in the habit of opening almost every pre-packaged article and putting it to immediate use, with no further action needed. It seems we carry that habit over to the meat we buy. We think that the "meat expert" who packaged it meant it to be just that way, and therefore it's ready to cook just as it is. We shouldn't tamper with it.

Not so!

Please consider:

- "Appearance is everything." The best side of the meat is always facing you. The worst side is not visible through the package. That isn't necessarily a bad thing, it's just that when you unwrap the meat, you may see more fat and/or bone than you counted on.

- It's your meat. Do with it what you will. Trim off the fat you may not want, take the bones out as you wish, separate the various separate muscles for various uses, etc. You can, for instance, take a couple of steaks from the eye of a Blade Cut Chuck Roast, and grind the rest for ground beef, cut it up for Carnitas or stew meat, or make a soup with the bones and tougher outer parts.

- If you want Rib Eye Steaks, but those on sale are "bone-in," just slide your knife along the bone and remove it.

- If you want New York Steaks, but Club Steaks are on sale at a cheaper price, slide your knife along the bone and remove the bone.

- If there's a large block of fat, slide your knife around the edge of it and remove it.

- Fat weighs about 18% less by volume than does muscle (meat). I never pass over a really great-looking cut of beef because it has excess fat. I'll remove whatever quantity of fat I don't want.

I simply slid my knife around the bones, removed them, and cut the "eye" portion into three beautiful boneless Chuck Eye Steaks. The single Boneless Rib Eye Steak labeled "Spencer" in the top photo, from the same meat counter, was $5.99 per pound. The price for the .74-pound steak was $4.43. Wouldn't you rather have the three bigger and better steaks than the "Spencer" for a total of forty-three cents more, plus almost one pound of lean trimmings for ground beef or however you might like to use them?

# About Aging Meat

When you let meat sit in a controlled temperature environment for ten to thirty days, this is called "aging." Aging allows enzymes in the meat to break down the tissues, making it more tender and improving the flavor.

Beef, venison, elk, moose and buffalo benefit by aging.

Pork, poultry, fish, and lamb and its relatives, such as Antelope and Mountain Sheep, are not "aged," but should be used as soon as possible or very tightly double wrapped in plastic food wrap and frozen. Pork, poultry and fish deteriorate relatively quickly, even under refrigeration. Lamb and its relatives will age, but the meat develops a strong, generally undesirable flavor the longer it's aged.

In aging beef for ten to fifteen days or more, at least a 10% loss of weight is usual. It's easy to see then why "dry aged" beef is more expensive, and not a common practice among retailers and supermarkets trying to sell their beef at the same or lower prices than their competitors. The cost of keeping the meat inventory under refrigeration, coupled with the inherent weight loss, adds so much to the cost that the retailer can't be competitive. The majority of the public aren't normally as interested in how much more tender or flavorful steak or roast might be, but in how much more it will cost to feed the family.

# Aging Beef

You can be sure that if you've ever eaten a shamefully expensive—but glorious—steak at a shamefully expensive—but glorious—restaurant, it had been dry aged, probably for around thirty days.

Any cut of beef benefits by aging. On those very rare occasions that I've ever bought a steak out of the counter, it's nearly always been from the discount section.

Usually the best steaks have been passed over until they've turned dark and have been discounted, often dramatically. They've turned dark, they're usually excessively fat, which of course can easily be removed, often very well marbled, and they're otherwise beautiful. Dark meat is often a matter of bacterial buildup. If that's the case, the bacteria are on the outside surface. After a second under a broiler or grill, they're deceased.

Any beef roast or steak brought home from the store should be immediately taken out of the store wrapping. It should be put on a plate or some such, only the top covered with a piece of plastic food wrap, and simply put in the refrigerator so that air can circulate around it. If your refrigerator stays at about 38° F, it will be fine for several days. If steaks begin to dry out, they should be used or tightly wrapped and frozen. A roast may develop a thin, dry, surface, which can be trimmed off either before or after cooking. Sometimes I'll give a roast a light rub of olive oil, cover it with seasonings, and just let it marinate for a week or so on a plate in the refrigerator. Primals of any sort can be and should be aged for a much longer period.

Ground meat of any kind can stay in the store package only for a day or so. If it isn't going to be used right away, as with any meat, it should be tightly double wrapped in plastic food wrap, put inside a thicker plastic bag or paper wrap, and frozen.

Dealers in premium beef, top-of-the-line restaurants and 4- and 5-star hotels primarily practice the aging of beef today. The purpose of aging beef is to make it the most tender it can be, and to fully bring out the flavor.

Aging beef, until somewhat recently, only meant a recently coined word, "dry aged."

With the invention and innovation of vacuum sealing primal cuts of meat in plastic wrap, the word, "wet aged" was coined. Wet aging refers to leaving the meat in vacuum-sealed plastic for a long period of time.

I'm not at all convinced that wet aging gives an honest product. Proponents of wet aging point out that there is no weight loss due to the drying effect inherent in the aging process. Otherwise they claim there's not much difference in the end product. That is an outrageous and false claim. The process of aging beef simply isn't accomplished when air can't reach the meat. Left in the plastic air-sealed package, there's no loss of weight. That's good for the retailer—if he can convince us that "wet-aged" is the same as "dry-aged." Beef is either aged or it isn't. Coining new words doesn't change the fact of the quality, tenderness and flavor of the steak on your plate.

Aging generally means that the beef, usually a hindquarter, is suspended from a large hook attached to a roller that rolls on a suspended rail in a walk-in cooler, which is kept at 38° F for a certain period of time. Primal cuts such as the Full Rib, Full Loin, Head Loin, or Short Loin are generally simply laid on a rack in a walk-in cooler or large refrigerator.

"Well aged" could mean almost anything. While some people insist that beef aged thirty days is ideal, it's the opinion of many that there is little to gain by aging it for more than ten days. After ten days, the beef should be very nearly as tender and flavorful as it will ever be, some say. I age our USDA Choice, Whole Boneless Beef Ribs or

Whole New York strips for twenty to thirty days. Virtually everyone who has had steaks that I've aged has proclaimed them "The best steak I've ever had."

As beef ages, a very thin layer of the exterior surface will become dry and hardened. If there is high humidity in the cooler, mold will develop. I've aged USDA Choice and Prime hindquarters for thirty days in a walk-in refrigerator with high humidity; they became overgrown with white mold that was three inches deep, sticking straight out like electrified hair. The outer layer of fat is going to be trimmed off in the usual cutting process, aged or not. The fact of a molded or dried thin surface is of no detriment or consequence at all, and there should never be any "off" flavor.

I simply take the primal, remove it from the plastic wrap, rinse it off, put it on a sheet of plastic coated "freezer wrap," plastic side up, on a shelf in the extra refrigerator.

*Rinsing a whole Sirloin Tip prior to cooling and/or aging*

I turn it over about once a week so it stays relatively dry on all sides. In three or four weeks, I'll cut it into steaks, tightly wrap them, put them in zip lock bags and use them when we want.

*The whole New York Strip (L) and the whole Boneless Rib had been aging for four or five days when the photo above was taken.*

## New York Strip Aged at Home

This USDA Choice, Whole New York Strip (or Top Loin Strip) was aged for about three weeks, as described above.

The amateurish and unskilled stripping of the exterior fat, which was done at the processing plant, can be seen in the next photo. There is 1½" of fat at one end, the meat was gouged into at the other end, and in various places the fat is removed right down to the meat itself.

*The top side of New York Strip after four weeks*

That this New York was packaged before the beef had completely cooled at the processing plant is obvious in the photo above. Had it been properly cooled, the exterior fat layer would be flat, even and smooth.

I would prefer to be able to buy primals with ½" to ¾" inch of fat left on the exterior. It can be easily trimmed off after aging and slicing, with no loss of meat. As the fat weighs 18% less than the meat, the cost would be of little consequence. The photo below is of the underside of the New York Strip/Top Loin Strip.

*The underside of the same New York Strip*

To ready the steaks for the grill or the freezer, I simply slice the steaks as thickly as I like, trim them of the excess fat, then trim off the outer dried surface of each steak.

*Slicing the aged New York Strip*

*Trimming the steaks as I go*

*A full set of steaks ready for trimming*

*Trimming the fat*

*Slicing off the paper-thin dried outer edge*

As can be seen below, these New York Steaks are just about as picture perfect and beautifully marbled as they get.

*Fully trimmed steaks with the pile of trimmings*

There is a sizable amount of trim, as can be seen. Only the thin, dried out, outer edge of meat is actually lost over non-aging. The fat would ordinarily have been trimmed prior to the steaks going in the meat counter, and the only weight loss in the aging process was water. As most of that water would quickly cook off when the steak was grilled or broiled, it isn't of much consequence.

## The Rib

Actually, the Rib Eye, as sold today, is nothing more than a Boneless Rib. The true "Eye of the Rib" doesn't include the tail. There is a triangular piece of fat at the base of the eye muscle, which contains another muscle, not as tender as the eye, but very marbled and tasty. It could be separated from the eye of the rib rather easily. The fatty meat at the base, the "tail," would have to be put into ground beef, or stew meat, as it would have no other value. Obviously, $18.95 per pound (or whatever the price of the steak) for the "tail" is good for the meat man. He'd have to charge a higher price for the rib eye if he couldn't leave the tail connected. As this is the standard way to sell a "Rib Eye," it's all calculated within the price. In the retail markets we always had a standard tail length for various steaks. For example, "Porterhouse Steaks should have a two-inch tail," and so forth.

Most chefs and meat experts agree that the Rib Steak, or Eye of the Rib Steak, is the most flavorful steak on the beef. It is usually preferred over the Short Loin Strip Steak, also known as New York Steak, or Shell Steak, or various other names. The Rib, being better marbled and having more fat than the Short Loin, is more flavorful for just that reason. As people generally want less fat, the Short Loin Steak/ New York Steak continues to be in greater demand— therefore higher priced—than the Rib Steak or Rib Eye Steak.

At Thanksgiving or Christmas, when demand is high for Standing Rib or Prime Rib Roasts, the price of a whole boneless Eye of the Rib might be 10–20% below the cost of a Bone-in Rib Roast.

Generally the Rib Eye is in the range of 10–20% less per pound than the New York Strip. "Prime Rib" used to mean that the beef the rib came from was graded USDA Prime. Technically, one can sell a USDA Standard graded beef rib as Prime without consequence. The honest way to name a beef rib roast that isn't graded USDA Prime is to call it a Standing Rib Roast. A retailer's integrity and credibility are questionable when they call a USDA Choice or USDA Select Standing Rib roast "Prime Rib."

Whenever I want to serve a Rib Roast, I simply cut off whatever size I need from a Boneless Rib Eye that I might have had aging just for that purpose. The last people I served such a roast to, both very fine home chefs, were amazed to think that you could actually make the best Prime Rib they said they had ever had, without the bones, as in a Standing Rib Roast. In addition to paying $1 less per pound without the bones that I'd throw away, the boneless rib is much easier to carve, and takes less time to cook.

**BEEF SECRETS straight from the BUTCHER**    *Lee O'Hara*

# Why Not Make Your Own?

The lower the fat content of the ground beef per the label, the better, we think.

"Ground Fresh Daily," the advertising says. It would be, in almost every case, more honest to say, "Re-Ground Fresh Daily."

## Fresh Ground Beef?

In most cases, the ground beef was first ground last week in Iowa, or some other distant state, stuffed in a long, large tube of plastic, and trucked to your local supermarket. We buy ground beef in Louisiana or Los Angeles this morning, after it's been re-ground and re-packaged into smaller packages. We don't need to know what kind of meat went into the grinder, do we? We don't need to know how long ago the meat was first ground, do we?

I do.

Want to have the best ground beef you ever tasted?

Grind your own.

Want to know that your ground beef is completely pure?

Grind your own.

Want to have the freshest, cleanest, tastiest ground beef money can buy?

Grind your own.

Want to feel safe eating your ground beef rare or medium-rare, rather than cooked to a cinder?

Grind your own.

Okay, so I grind my own—what do I grind, and how do I do that anyway?

## Real Homemade Ground Beef Versus Store-Bought

*(L) 22% fat ground beef from store;*
*(C) homemade ground beef;*
*(R) 30% fat ground beef from store*

The package on the left is "Fresh Ground Beef," Lean, less than 22% fat. At 1.12 pounds at $2.99, the cost is $3.35. The package on the right above is "Fresh Ground Beef," less than 30% fat. At 1.12 pounds for $2.09 , the total cost is $2.34.

Our homemade ground beef, in the center, for 1.12 pounds, at $2.39, would cost a total of $2.68.

What can you grind? You don't have to be a meat expert to make homemade ground beef.

I try to buy the cuts of meat we use the most on sale. For our tastes, we prefer our ground beef to be juicy, which means it has to have some fat content. Additionally, because we prefer it a little coarser, we grind the meat only once, using the medium-sized grinding plate.

| **NOTE:** Since the meat is then a little coarser, it tends to break apart in the frying pan or grill. The simple solution for that is to dissolve ½ teaspoon of salt in ½ cup of water, pour it over two or three meat, stir it in, and let it rest in the refrigerator for an hour or more. Salt breaks down the cell walls, and the patties will now hold their shape.

If you prefer your ground beef finer, you would use the medium sized meat grinding plate, and then re-grind it through the smallest sized meat grinding plate, which is the way it is done commercially.

Boneless chuck roasts or whole boneless chucks are often on sale and can be bought for about $2 per pound. I'll buy whatever total weight I want, sometimes buying four or five roasts of three to six pounds each.

For homemade ground beef, most of us wouldn't want to use USDA Choice beef, as the fat within the meat, called marbling, can't be removed. With no lean meat to add to Choice trimmings, the fat content of the ground beef is high.

Most supermarkets today carry the next lower grade, but call it by some trade name, such as someone's special "Reserve" or some such. USDA Select is generally ideal for making your own ground beef as the fat content is enough to make the ground beef juicy without it being overly fat.

After you've ground your own beef a time or two, you'll know what fat content your family prefers. Generally USDA Select or ungraded beef works very well—in the case of ground beef, the fresher it is ground and used the better it is. Nothing you can buy in a meat market will compare to any beef you grind an hour or two before you use it.

I would never hand the meat man a piece of meat and ask him to grind it for me, because:

- Is the grinder auger, blade, plate and tray clean?

- If the grinder and all its parts weren't washed since its last use, what was the last thing run through the grinder? Was it lamb, pork or…?

If the grinder hadn't been washed since its last use, some of the last meat that was ground is still in the auger, wrapped around the cutting blade, and the grinding plate is solidly packed with whatever it was. The first thing to come out of the grinder, in front of your meat, is whatever was at the tail end of whatever was ground last. You're going to get that, and the tail end of your meat is going to go into whatever is ground next in that grinder.

## Grinding Your Own

1. Purchase the meat.

2. Cut the meat into strips for easy grinding.

3. Set up your grinder.

4.   Feed the meat one slice at a time into the grinder.

5.   Use the meat pusher on the smaller pieces of meat.

6.   Weigh out six-ounce portions (or any size you prefer).

7.    Press each portion into a patty and place on cookie sheet.

Put the patties in the freezer for an hour to let them chill.

8.    After an hour, remove the patties from the freezer, double-wrap in clear plastic wrap (see "How to Wrap Meat" on page 132.) then place in an airtight zip lock bag or other airtight container. Once wrapped, they can be frozen for future use.

## Finding the Right Grinder

There is a variety of home meat-grinding machines available, from manual ones you clamp to a table top, to various tabletop electric grinders. The cheaper plastic meat grinder models cost around $40.00, and the stainless steel and cast iron electric meat grinders that should last a lifetime run about $100.

Nobody new to grinding meat should buy the plastic and Teflon models. The problem is that the parts are flexible, which causes jamming, which in turn causes one to have to stop and fix the problem with regularity. I fought with and wore out two meat grinders over the years until I finally found that really good steel and cast-iron meat grinders were available. I've not had a jam or any other problem since using this type of meat grinder.

I make a lot of sausages and salamis for friends and family, plus whatever hamburger the family wants, and have probably used my meat grinder more in three years than most people would in a lifetime. It's still like new and turns grinding meat from being a chore into a fun and easy thing to do.

*Assembled meat grinder with the meat pusher in the tray*

This kind of electric meat grinder is available for about $100. I bought this one from www.sausagemaker.com for $99. I've had it for about three years, and with the use it gets, which is an average of forty to sixty pounds a month I expect it will last at least another fifty years with proper care. This meat grinder is a joy to work with.

The plastic and Teflon meat grinder this one replaced cost about $40, and I struggled with it for many years. I don't recommend the plastic models, especially for the inexperienced. They can be a challenge to work with, often needing to be cleaned in the middle of grinding meat. The initial savings is quickly forgotten in lost time, lost meat, and hair-pulling frustration.

*Meat grinder parts, ready for assembly,*
*(L–R): Locking Ring, Grinding Plate ($3/_{16}$" holes),*
*Cutting Blade, Auger, Grinder Head*

*Meat grinder head, with auger,
cutting blade and grinding plate*

This kind of grinder usually comes with three grinder plates: small holes about ⅛", medium holes about $^3/_{16}$", and large holes about ¼".

*Three cutting plates: small, medium and large holes*

*Fully assembled meat grinder head*

*Slipping the assembled meat grinder head into the base*

Commercially, beef is generally ground once through about a $^3/_{16}$" plate, and then through the ⅛" plate. This serves several purposes, the main being that it ensures the fat and red meat are well mixed together.

If you use good quality meat and take out the heavy gristle, tendons, bone particles, blood clots, and other obnoxious little things the commercial guys don't have time to bother with, then you only need to grind it once.

*Ready for the meat tray*

*Ready for the meat*

*Meat pusher poised and ready to push!*

## Taking the Meat Grinding Machine Head Apart for Cleaning

**NOTE:** For safety, *always* turn the grinder off *and* disconnect the power cord before disassembling!

1. Remove the locking ring with plastic wrench.

*After a quick switch on and off for an easy release of auger, cutting blade and grinding plate.*

2.   Clean the locking ring.

| **NOTE:** When washing steel and cast iron grinder parts, be sure to wash and *immediately dry* those parts that can rust. Rust will form quickly if the parts are not fully dried. Properly maintained, your grinder should last a lifetime.

## Trouble?

If you have trouble with the meat mashing, rather than perfect grinding, it's almost always a matter of the cutting plate coming out of the notch in the grinder head.

*Place the meat-grinding plate over the cutting blade with notch in cutting plate in proper position.*

The notch in the plate must fit into the little knob in the head of the grinder for it to remain stationary.

# What is Freezer Burn?

From my observations over the years, it appears we could feed Nebraska and New York with the food we throw out every week because of "freezer burn."

Freezer burn is simply the dehydration of any food, be it meat, vegetable, fruit or baked goods. Many people don't realize that ice evaporates in a freezer. Sometimes you find that the ice cubes in the ice cube tray are about half the size they should be. The tray was full when it went into the freezer. The ice cubes evaporated. Today's "frost free" freezers and refrigerators take the moisture out of the air in the freezer, but they also take the moisture out of anything that isn't tightly wrapped or sealed. This causes what we call "freezer burn."

The same evaporation process happens with meat that isn't sealed in an air-tight wrapping. The moisture in the meat evaporates; leaving only desiccated reddish or white fibrous cell walls that weigh a tiny fraction of the original food. If only the surface of the meat freezer burned, the tainted taste of the remaining meat makes it pretty much inedible.

## Popular Myths

In chatting with good friends over lunch recently, I was surprised to learn that freezer burn was a long time problem for them. My friends mentioned that every few weeks they discover something in their freezer that they'd forgotten about and now had to throw it out because it was freezer-burned. They had just thrown out two large packages of boneless chicken breasts with freezer burn.

"How long had it been in the freezer?"

"Three, maybe four weeks," they answered.

"How could that be?"

"Oh, you know, you think you'll use it, then you don't, so you throw it in the freezer."

"And how did you wrap it before "'throwing it in the freezer?'"

"It was already wrapped," they told me.

You can't do that. They didn't know there was anything to know about freezing meat. It is possible to freeze meat, or any food, the right way, and not have freezer burn.

Meats in the meat counter are minimally wrapped. Such meats are intended to be used while fresh. It isn't intended for meat to be frozen in those wrappings.

## It Is Possible to Stop Freezer Burn

If you're going to freeze food and avoid freezer burn, the meat must be fully and tightly sealed. I sometimes run across steaks, homemade blocks of Eggplant Parmesan, a Chuck Roast that I'd made into corned beef or Pastrami, and sundry other foodstuffs in the freezer compartments of our refrigerators that have sat for two years or more, without a trace of freezer burn, seemingly as fresh as the day they went into the freezer.

## How to Wrap Meat

The following method is called a "roll wrap." After you've wrapped two or three packages, you'll be an expert.

As a historical note, there was also a "drug store wrap" that some locker plants used. The drug store wrap made a neater looking package, but it took a bit longer and wasn't practical except in wrapping hamburger, or somewhat square and rectangular cuts of meat.

1.  Take off any and all store wrappings.

2.  Starting out at the bottom left-hand corner of the plastic food wrap, place the larger end of the meat to the right, as in the photo.

3.  Tightly pull the corner of the plastic wrap over the meat, while holding the wrap down with the other hand.

4.  Fold the plastic wrap tightly against the right edge of the meat and pull the lower right hand corner of the wrap over the meat.

5.   While maintaining a tight pressure, roll the meat forward one turn.

6.   Tightly fold the left side of the wrap against the meat and tightly pull the wrap over the meat.

7.   Roll the package forward while maintaining a tight seal at both ends.

8. Re-do exactly the same process, giving it a double wrap, starting now from the opposite end of the package.

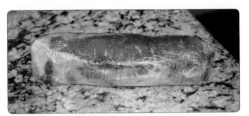

*The finished product!*

The finished product is now tightly sealed and no air will be able to circulate around it, eliminating the possibility of freezer burn and wasted food dollars. Notice that the plastic wrap is self-sealing and there is no need to tape or otherwise secure the end of the wrap.

To further protect the now double-wrapped package from being punctured, or the seal created by the plastic wrap to become undone or broken, the package should be protected.

We like to use a self-sealing bag, being sure to squeeze out any air before zipping it closed. A double-wrapped package can also be wrapped in butcher paper or put inside a brown paper bag, or into almost anything that will protect the package.

You can use the same wrapping technique to wrap two or more cuts of meat together.

*Two steaks wrapped together*

*Two steaks wrapped together*

# Aluminum Foil

Some research has been done over the last many years that indicates the element aluminum accumulates in the brain, and may be a significant cause of Alzheimer's disease and similar brain dysfunctions. If you've ever wrapped food, especially salty food or meat, directly in aluminum foil and left in the freezer for a month or two, you may have seen how pitted the aluminum foil was when the food was unwrapped. The aluminum has dissolved into the food. Since having first observed that and tasted the metallic flavor of the food, I've never done it again. It wasn't brain damage I feared, and this was decades before any such research was done; it was simply the awful metallic flavor of the food.

I use as much aluminum foil as anyone in cooking. First, however, I wrap the food very thoroughly in parchment paper so that aluminum can't come into direct contact with the food. Over hot coals, the outer parchment paper will severely char, so I may give it two or three wraps before wrapping it with aluminum. After double wrapping tightly in plastic food wrap, meat can be wrapped in aluminum foil, zip-lock bags, brown paper bags, or anything else to further protect the plastic wrap from tearing. A hole in the plastic wrapped meat, where air has access to the meat, will defeat the purpose.

When using an aluminum pan in the oven, I cover the bottom of the pan with parchment paper before putting any food on it. The normal kindling temperature of paper is 451⁰ F. There's nothing I would cook at that temperature in the oven, so I never have to worry about it catching fire.

# BEEF SECRETS straight from the BUTCHER    *Lee O'Hara*

# Sharpen Your Knife

It seems most people have a drawer full of knives, all too dull to work with.

Poor-quality steel won't hold an edge. A knife made of poor-quality steel can be very sharp when you buy it, and under normal kitchen use, quickly become dull. It will be fast and easy to sharpen, and it will be fast and easy to make it dull again. A blade made of high-quality steel will stay sharp for a long time, but it will take much longer to sharpen good steel than it takes to sharpen poor steel.

I've had two knives, all anyone really needs, that I've cut millions of pounds of meat with over the last fifty years. They're both made by the Swiss company, Forschner, and with proper care, it appears they could easily be given the same use for another 100 years. The larger of the two is a "steak knife" with a ten-inch blade, the other is a "boning knife" with a six-inch blade. I've seen many knives used for two full generations of meat men that looked like they could easily last another generation or two.

Both my knives are always sharp enough to shave with. Meat cutters know that a dull knife is more dangerous to work with. Because you have to apply more force and pressure with a dull knife to what you're cutting, accidents are more likely. With a sharp knife you aren't pushing, tugging and doing unusual motions to get the job done. The blade slides through the meat easily.

In my youth when I first began to sharpen some knives for friends and relatives, the first thing they wanted to do was to cut themselves badly enough to require stitches. Since then I haven't sharpened a knife for someone else without first making them endure my harangue about knife safety—and make them swear an oath to follow what I said:

- It's impossible to cut yourself if you or your hands aren't in front of the blade—never have your hand or fingers below or in front of anywhere near where the blade is going.

- Be certain the meat you're going to cut is stable and on a solid and stable surface. If the meat rolls, slips or slides, or the surface you're working on moves, you could suddenly find you or your fingers in front of an on-coming blade.

- Be fully aware of your work area and don't allow yourself to get distracted by anything. If you have to tend to the kids, put the knife down and come back when that's done. You should be doing one thing only when working with a sharp knife—working with a sharp knife.

- Good knives should be hand-washed only, one at a time. The heat of a dishwasher is too high for the steel, and if it has a wooden handle, it will ruin the finish as well as deteriorate the wood.

- A knife with a straight blade should always be laid flat on it's side. Putting it down for a moment with the sharp edge straight up is hazardous.

- When washing a knife, as in working with a knife, do nothing but wash one knife. Never put sharp knives in the sink with other dishes. You can pretty much count on cutting yourself if you do that. Immerse the knife in the hot soapy water, take it out and run the sponge along the blade, from the top of the blade toward the point only. Never draw the sponge back toward yourself along the blade.

*Never put sharp knives in the sink with other dishes.*

*Run the sponge along the blade, from the top of the blade toward the point only. Never draw the sponge back toward yourself along the blade.*

## Knife Sharpening

There are dozens of knife-sharpening techniques, but probably the oldest and best is simply rubbing the blade across a sharpening stone. Any technique is right if it results in a sharpened knife and doesn't damage the blade.

No knife blade to be used for meat should ever get near an electric sharpener or grinder. Invariably, even so-called professional knife sharpeners burn the steel, effectively ruining the blade. Thereafter it won't hold an edge, and you'll start seeing little chips in the blade.

## Sharpening Tools

If you're only going to have one sharpening tool, it should be a stone. If you have two, the second should be a steel.

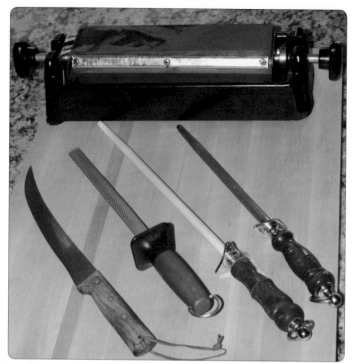

*(Top) A sharpening stone; (Bottom, L–R): Much used fifty-year-old knife with a 10" blade, a diamond sharpener, a ceramic sharpener, and a steel*

The stone pictured above actually has three different stones: coarse, medium and fine. This is a commercial stone, but way more stone than most people would ever need or want to invest in. I very rarely use anything but the fine stone.

## Sharpening Stones

Sharpening stones aren't expensive, and are readily available. They are typically two-sided: coarse on one side and fine on the other.

### A Common Method for Stone

The most common technique used by meat cutters is probably this one:

1. To begin, I lay the knife on the stone, with the handle nearest the stone, and with almost no angle at all between the blade and the stone, and simply draw the blade along the stone toward the point. I use a very small amount of sewing machine oil on the stone to keep it from cutting too deeply into the steel.

I'm very careful in holding the knife point, only applying enough pressure to ensure the blade remains in contact with the stone during the stroke. In the beginning, I advise slow strokes.

**CAUTION:** I have a couple of scars from letting my fingers slip off the knife point and encounter the oncoming blade. I use a light touch and keep the oil off my fingers and the blade as much as possible.

2.    Then I turn the blade over, being sure that I have exactly the same angle between the blade and the stone as I used on the other side, and draw it back across the stone in exactly the same way.

Depending on how dull the knife was, it may take from two to three minutes to touch it up, or longer if it was really dull. I just don't let our kitchen knives get very dull to begin with.

Very high quality steel holds its edge for a very long time. The blade in the photos, which I've cut a few million pounds of meat with, has been sharpened hundreds of times. As can be seen, very little of the original steel has been worn away.

# Steel Sharpener

A steel is helpful if it's properly used. It takes no metal off the blade, as does a stone or ceramic sharpener. It makes the blade sharper by straightening the finest edge and by aligning the positive and negative electrons. Steels are magnetized just for that purpose. If a steel loses its magnetism, it isn't effective.

*This magnetized steel knife sharpener can pick up keys.*

Like a good knife, a good steel should last for generations of use. When not in use, they shouldn't be stored where they are in contact with other metal.

## Using a Steel

As with the stone, the most important thing about sharpening a blade is to keep as exactly the same angle on each side of the blade as strokes are made.

There should be almost no discernible angle, and the blade appears almost flat as it's drawn down the steel. It's drawn once down on one side of the blade, then once down the other side of the blade, back and forth.

The hand holding the steel (or ceramic) should remain absolutely stationary, and the only movement should be from the wrist as the blade is drawn along the steel.

Four or five strokes on each side are all that's really useful.

You'll find:

- The better the quality of the steel in the blade, the longer it will hold an edge and stay sharp.

- It will also take much longer to get the edge back after it gets dull.

## Diamond and Ceramic Sharpeners

If you have a diamond or ceramic sharpening tool, it's used either before or after the steel.

The diamond sharpener and ceramic sharpener are relatively new sharpening tools, coming on the scene only in the past thirty to forty years. They are used exactly the same as the steel, and remove a very small amount of steel. I use the ceramic sharpener almost every time I use a knife, as it keeps a very fine edge on the blade. I usually don't need to use the stone but about every two or three years.

I've often sharpened knives for friends. Generally they're fine looking, somewhat expensive knives—of very poor steel. I'm always embarrassed when they rave about how sharp I got them. It takes less than five minutes to sharpen a handful of knives made of poor quality steel.

## Front Quarter

| Primal | Cut | Notes and Comments |
|---|---|---|
| **Rib** | Rib Steak | Also called Bone-in Rib Eye Steak |
| | Standing Rib Roast | |
| | Boneless Rib Eye Roast | |
| | Standing Rib Roast (bone in) | |
| | Rib Eye Steak | Also called Spencer Steak, Delmonico Steak, Boneless Rib Eye Steak |
| **Brisket and Plate** | Brisket Point | |
| | Brisket Plate | Also called Flat Plate |
| | Skirt Steak | Also called Pinwheel Steak (rolled up with a skewer through it) |
| **Chuck and Neck** | Blade Cut Chuck Roast | |
| | 7-Bone Chuck Roast | If you don't see the "7" bone in a 7-Bone Roast, it's either a mislabeled Blade Cut Chuck Roast, or it's Neck. The Neck is very lean and should be made into ground beef, or cooked long and slow. A good Blade Cut Chuck Roast or a good 7_Bone Roast may be suitable as an oven roast, but the neck never would be. |
| | Chuck Steak | |
| | Eye of Chuck Steak | |
| | Flat Iron Steak | |
| | Flat Iron Roast | |
| | Chuck Filet | |
| **Cross Rib** | Cross Rib Steak | Also called Shoulder Clod Steak |
| | Cross Rib Roast | Also called Shoulder Clod Roast |
| | English Cut Short Ribs | |
| **Shank** | Shank | Front Shank and Rear Shank are almost indistinguishable |

# Beef Cuts Chart

## Hindquarter

| Primal | Cut | Notes and Comments |
|---|---|---|
| **Shank** | Shank | Front Shank and Rear Shank are almost indistinguishable |
| **Short Loin** | Porterhouse Steak | |
| | T-Bone Steak (without the Filet) | Also called Bone-in New York Steak, Bone-in Shell Steak, Top Loin Steak, Bone-in Top Loin Steak, Club Steak |
| | New York Strip (boneless) | Also called Top Loin Strip |
| | New York Steak | Also called Top Loin Steak, Boneless New York Steak, Shell Steak |
| **Round** | Top Round Steak | Also called London Broil |
| | Bottom Round Steak | |
| | Bottom Round Roast | |
| | Eye of Round Steak | Also called Breakfast Steak |
| | Eye of Round Roast | |
| **Sirloin Tip** | Sirloin Tip Steak | |
| | Sirloin Tip Roast | |
| | Tri-Tip | |
| **Head Loin** | Top Sirloin Steak | |
| | Top Sirloin Roast | |
| | Filet | Also called Filet Mignon (The Filet sits within both the Head Loin and the Short Loin primals) |
| **Flank** | Flank Steak | |
| | Flap Meat | Often seasoned and called Carne Asada |

Don't be led astray by a flowery name on the label. Know what primal it came from, and you have a good idea what it can best be used for.

# Wrapping It Up

Only the last 10% of modern man's history has included growing our own food, both crops and herds of domesticated animals. Until only about 10,000 years ago, if a man didn't want his family to die, he had to procure meat.

Fast-forwarding up to today, we've become so specialized that most of us have one or two skills and must depend on other specialists for almost all of our daily requirements.

Those of us who are omnivorous buy our meat from the market and trust that it's been well handled.

What do we know about the nine ounces of meat they say we eat every day? After reading this book, you know a great deal more than most, and knowledge is power.

My intention in writing this book was to increase your understanding, and with that, your ability to have more control over an important part of your daily life. I hope you now understand enough to have better beef on your table for less money.

Thank you for joining me!

# Acknowledgements

Nobody has ever written anything that wasn't a reflection of his or her life experience as influenced, assisted and modified by friends and associates. When I had the idea to write on this subject and started asking people their thoughts on the need for such a book, I received nothing but encouragement. My friends are not the kind who'll tell me pink is yellow just to keep me happy. In fact they can be rather brutal with my feelings. And I deeply thank each and every one of them who made suggestions, comments and biting criticisms along the way.

Very special thanks and appreciation go to:

- Mike and Barbara Lee, who welcomed me to use their world-class home and chef's dream kitchen for photo shoots and demonstrations.

- The beautiful work of photographer Chris Alvarado, who dropped many more important things whenever I had any photo need that just couldn't wait.

- Barbara Lee, highly skilled photographer being just one of her many accomplishments, for some last minute photo work. Her photo editing mastery continues to amaze me and made this an easier endeavor that it had any right to be.

- Our office manager, Gretchen Barnes, who found my lost files, located my missing photos, and kept me from throwing my computer through the window on any number of occasions. By her keeping my more graphic manner and baser inclinations under control this is no doubt an easier book to read.

- Wife Melissa for enduring my many fits and frustrations in trying to get it right.

- Alexander's Prime Meats, within Howie's Ranch Market, San Gabriel, CA, freely welcomed us into their market. I had begun to despair in ever finding whole quarters of beef that I could get photographed. It was a complete pleasure to again be able see the ultimate quality in meats being sold from old time meat counters by true professionals. I thought the day of the real meat-cutter had all but passed.

- And finally, thanks to my editor, Su Falcon. Only those who saw the disconnected twisted and gnarled pages I gave her could fully appreciate her mastery.

# Index

Debt load getting to you? Feeling financial pressure? Ready to toss your credit cards? Get tips on how to survive today's economy.

www.ConciseGuidelines.com

for ideas on how to:

- ◆ manage your money
- ◆ understand credit card charges
- ◆ get out of debt and stay that way!